Student Book

Blueprint

2

A1+ Elementary

Eric Williams · Natalie Ryan

Contents

* Also, see the glossary in the back of the Workbook.

Contents

Grammar and Structures	Listening / Reading	Writing / Speaking
Lesson 1 Comparison with adjectives **Lesson 2** Review of *-ing* forms and introduction to *-ing* adjectives **Lesson 3** *How* + adjective questions and answers **Lesson 4** Superlative adjectives **Lesson 5** Linking verbs	**R**&**L**: Recommendations about moving and classes to take **R**&**L**: Directions to an apartment for rent **R**: An apartment ad **R**: A chart comparing apartments for rent **R**&**L**: Feelings about things that are happening **R**: Reading a map and a map legend	**S**: Talking about your commute **S**&**W**: Descriptions of what's happening **S**&**W**: Describing the location of your home or workplace in words and with maps **S**&**W**: Making up a story **S**: Calling about apartments for rent **S**: Giving directions
Lesson 1 Simple past of *be* **Lesson 2** *there was/were*; conjunctions *or* and *but* **Lesson 3** Prepositional phrases of time (*in / on / at*) **Lesson 4** Simple past (regular verbs) and past time expressions **Lesson 5** Simple past (irregular verbs)	**R**&**L**: Conversations about a new apartment, a visit with a friend, a neighborhood, movies, and everyday routines **R**: Reading a map **R**: Reading a postcard **R**&**L**: A movie schedule **R**: Reading a planner entry **L**: Descriptions and comparison of apartments	**W**&**S**: Comparing old and new apartments **S**: Talking about where you lived in the past **S**: Describing a place **W**&**S**: Describing daily and weekly routines **W**&**S**: Describing your old house or apartment **W**&**S**: Describing your dream house
Lesson 1 Making suggestions with *let's* + verb or *What about / How about* + verb + *-ing* **Lesson 2** Discussing the future; showing agreement **Lesson 3** *can* for ability; *can* and *could* for possibility **Lesson 4** *can* for offers and volunteering; *need to* for obligation **Lesson 5** Imperatives	**R**&**L**: Conversations about trip possibilities, preferences, plans, preparation, and booking **R**: Ads for travel destinations **R**: An email exchange about booking a trip **R**: A diagram of the inside of an airplane **L**: A conversation between a travel agent and a customer	**W**&**S**: Suggesting travel destinations **W**&**S**: Writing and talking about likes, dislikes, and future plans **S**: Deciding on a travel partner, where to go, and what to do **W**&**S**: Making a to-do list **S**: Talking to a travel agent **W**&**S**: A travel flyer **W**&**S**: Writing notes and using them to speak about adventure tours
Lesson 1 *can* and *could* for offers and requests **Lesson 2** Questions with *whose* and possessive pronouns **Lesson 3** Comparing with adverbs **Lesson 4** Superlative adverbs; *how* + adverb **Lesson 5** *have* + O + *to* verb	**R**&**L**: Getting directions in an airport **R**&**L**: Conversations at a check-in counter, security, and an airport gate **R**: A dictionary entry **R**&**L**: A conversation between a passenger and airport ground staff **R**: FAQs on a website **R**: A departure board	**S**: Making offers and requests **S**: Discussing how to pack a suitcase **W**: Listing things you can't take on a plane **S**: Asking questions about a trip **S**: Talking about a past trip **S**: Calling an airline agent **W**: Diagramming the airport process

First Conversations

Module 1 Goals

Understand and use words and phrases about family, personal details, and simple everyday situations

Communicate information about yourself, your family, your job, and where you come from in a simple and direct exchange

Describe your family simply (for example, who the members are, how old they are, and what they do)

Understand when people talk very slowly and clearly about themselves and their families, using simple words

Build a basic vocabulary of words and phrases to talk about yourself and communicate in common everyday situations

Write simply about simple topics, such as the weather

Join phrases with words like *and* or *because*

Correctly use some simple structures that you have memorized

Preview

Look at pages 8 to 33. What pages are these things on?

a handshake _____

Albert Einstein _____

words related to weather _____

pictures of long bridges _____

Write and Discuss

Write your answers to the questions. Then talk about them with a partner.

1. In your country, what do people do when they meet someone for the first time?

2. What do you think "small talk" means?
   I think "small talk"…

3. What do strangers in your country talk about—for example, at a bus stop?
   They usually talk about …

4. Do your friends have jobs? If so, what are their jobs?

5. What English words do you know to talk about weather?

Unit 1

Unit 2

Scan the QR code to watch a preview video.

| Lesson 1 | Nice to meet you. |

A Model Conversation

Read the conversation. Then listen. ⊙ Track 02

Woman: Hi, Dad. It's so good to see you!

Dad: Hey, Teri. Yeah, it's good to be here.

Teri: This is my friend Chad. He's here at the train station with me because he's going out of town. His friend is getting married this afternoon.

Dad: Oh, okay. It's nice to meet you, Chad.

Chad: Nice to meet you too, Mr. Dunbar.

Dad: Please, call me Tony.

Teri: Thanks for the ride, Chad. We're heading to lunch, but let's get together after you get back. Good seeing you!

Chad: Yeah, see you later. Nice meeting you, Tony.

B Vocabulary

Read the conversation again. Match the expressions to the correct definitions.

1. Good to see you. •
2. Nice to meet you. •
3. Nice meeting you. •

4. Good seeing you. •
5. This is… •
6. train station •
7. get married •
8. head •
9. get together •

10. Thanks for the ride. •

• a. to become someone's husband or wife
• b. a phrase used to introduce a person to another person
• c. a phrase used to end a conversation with someone you are meeting for the first time
• d. a place to get on or off of a train
• e. a phrase used to greet someone you know
• f. a phrase used to thank someone for bringing you in a car
• g. to go
• h. a phrase used to end a conversation with someone you know
• i. a phrase used to greet someone you are meeting for the first time
• j. to meet a friend; to meet someone socially

C Vocabulary in Context

Fill in the blanks to complete the conversation. Listen and check. Then practice with a partner. ⊙ Track 03

Jane: Hey, Greg! ❶ _____ _____ _____ _____ again! How are you?

Greg: Hi, Jane. Good to see you, too. ❷ _____ _____ my girlfriend, Beth.

Beth: ❸ _____ _____ meet you.

Jane: Nice to meet you, too.

Greg: Actually, Beth and I are going to ❹ _____ _____ next year.

Jane: Wow, congratulations!

Greg: Yeah, thanks. Anyway, where are you ❺ _____?

Jane: Downtown—I'm getting ❻ _____ with a friend.

Greg: Oh. We are, too. Do you want a ride?

Jane: No, thanks. I'm riding my bike. ❼ _____ _____ _____, Beth.

Beth: You too.

Greg: ❽ _____ _____ _____ again, Jane.

D Grammar

Subject pronouns and be

Brief note

Contractions such as *I'm* can be used in long answers and statements but not in short answers. Don't just say, "Yes, I'm." Say, "Yes, I am," or, "Yes, I'm a student."

be questions	short answers	long answers and statements
Am I a boy?	Yes, I **am**. / No, **I'm not**.	Yes, **I'm** a boy. / No, **I'm not** a boy.
Is he / she / it nice?	Yes, he / she / it **is**. No, he / she / it **isn't**. No, **he's** / **she's** / **it's not**.	Yes, **he's** / **she's** / **it's** nice. No, he / she / it **isn't** nice. No, **he's** / **she's** / **it's not** nice.
Are you / we / they hungry?	Yes, you / we / they **are**. No, you / we / they **aren't**.	Yes, you / we / they **are** hungry. No, you / we / they **aren't** hungry.

E Grammar Practice

Brief note

There are other contractions, too: *you're*, *we're*, and *they're*.

Fill in the blanks with subject pronouns, forms of *be*, or contractions.

1. Q: Are _____ European?   A: No, I'm _____. _____ not European.
2. Q: _____ that the train station?   A: Yes, it _____. _____ the train station.
3. Q: _____ _____ siblings?   A: No, they _____. _____ not siblings.
4. Q: _____ I late for the train?   A: Yes, _____ late for the train.
5. Q: _____ _____ raining today?   A: No, _____ _____ raining.
6. Q: _____ you Elle's sister?   A: Yes, _____ Elle's sister. Nice to meet you.

F Listen to Speak

Listen and circle the correct answers. Then guess the person. Write your answer—don't say it. 🔘 Track 04

1. This person (is / isn't) a basketball player.
2. This person (is / isn't) a soccer player.
3. This person (is / isn't) from the UK.
4. This person (does / doesn't) play for a Spanish team.

Who is it? _____

G Use the Language

Twenty questions

Play the guessing game from part F, "twenty questions," with a partner. Each partner thinks of a famous or known person (actor, teacher, friend, etc.) and then tries to guess the other player's person by asking yes/no questions. Try to guess correctly in twenty questions or less. The person who guesses after the fewest questions wins, so don't forget to count the questions!

When you're finished, write down the names of your person and your partner's person. Then tell the class.

My person:	My partner's person:

Practice the game again with another partner.

9

How are you doing?

A Model Conversation

Read the conversation. Then listen. 🔘 Track 05

Man: Hi. You're Wendy, right? How are you?

Wendy: I'm great, thanks. Are you the reporter from the school newspaper?

Man: That's right. I'm Jason. Nice to meet you. Sorry I'm late. Do you still have time to talk?

Wendy: Sure. I go to work at 2:00, and it's 12:30 now.

Jason: Okay. And can we talk here, or should we go to a coffee shop?

Wendy: It's a beautiful day. Let's just sit here.

Jason: All right. I just want to ask you a few questions about the cooking contest. Congratulations on winning, by the way. So first, where do you work?

Wendy: Well, I'm a student, and I also have a part-time job as a barista.

Jason: Oh, that's surprising. The winner is usually a professional cook. How old are you, if you don't mind my asking?

Wendy: I'm 19. Cooking is my future job. I want to own a restaurant someday.

> **Brief note**
> Use the phrase "if you don't mind my asking" when you ask a personal question.

B Vocabulary

Read the conversation again. Match the expressions to the correct definitions. 🔘 Track 05

1. professional	•	• a.	a person who cooks as a job or hobby
2. contest	•	• b.	large pieces of paper with news and advertisements
3. win	•	• c.	a phrase used to change the topic of a conversation
4. newspaper	•	• d.	happening at a time after now
5. own	•	• e.	doing a job that needs special education or skills
6. reporter	•	• f.	an event in which people try to do something better than others
7. cook	•	• g.	a person who writes news, often for a newspaper
8. future	•	• h.	to be the best in a game, contest, etc.
9. by the way	•	• i.	to have; to possess
10. congratulations	•	• j.	a word used to tell someone that you are happy about their good luck or success

C Vocabulary: How are you?

Study the answers to the questions "How are you?" or "How are you doing?" Then fill in the blanks.

I'm...	fine	sick	okay	well	great

Worst ◄- -► Best

1. tired	3. not bad	6. good / _____	7. awesome
2. _____	4. _____	8. _____
	5. _____ / all right	

Now ask two partners how they are today and tell them how you are.

be with *how* and adjectives; empty *it*

be in how questions		empty it	
how + be + subject	How **are** you? How **is** your mother? How **am** I doing?	Sentences about weather, times, days, dates, and distances often have an **empty it** subject. It's "empty" because it doesn't replace a noun.	
How *far / long / much / many / old* *+ be + S*	How long **is** the movie? How far **is** the store? How much **is** it? How old **are** you?	weather	A: How's the weather? B: **It's** a beautiful day. **It's** sunny.
adjectives after *be*		time	A: What time is **it**? B: **It's** 2:00.
subject + *be* + adjective	She**'s** beautiful. We**'re** awesome. I**'m** hungry.	day/date	A: What day is **it**? / What's the date? B: **It's** Monday. / **It's** July 23.
		distance	A: How far is **it** to campus? B: **It's** two kilometers.

E **Grammar Practice**

Match the answers to the questions.

1. You're doing well. •
2. It's two hours long. •
3. She's great. •
4. I'm 20. •
5. It's okay. •
6. It's $25. •

• **a.** How is your dinner?
• **b.** How much is the pizza?
• **c.** How old are you?
• **d.** How long is the movie?
• **e.** How am I reading?
• **f.** How's your grandmother?

Write a question for each answer.

7. The theater is five miles away. How _____?
8. He's six feet five inches. How _____?
9. The show is three hours long. _____?
10. It's Friday. _____?
11. It's raining. _____?
12. It's March 14th. _____?
13. It's half past one. _____?

F **Read to Speak**

Work with a partner. Take turns reading the roles of the man and the woman in the conversation in part A. The partner playing the woman replaces the woman's information with details about his or her own life.

Present one of your conversations to the class.

A Model Conversation

Read the conversation. Then listen. 🔴 Track 06

Man: Hi, Tammy. Who's this? Oh, right. We have a new employee today. What's your name?

Tammy: Tony, this is Nick Johnson, our summer intern. Nick, this is Tony Hendricks. He's the office secretary.

Nick: Nice to meet you, Tony.

Tony: Welcome to the company.

Tammy: Here Nick, have a seat. This is Elaine Rodriguez, and that's our supervisor, Stacy Ramon.

Nick: Nice to meet both of you.

Stacy: Glad to meet you too. How's your first day going?

Nick: I like my coworkers, but I'm still finding my way around.

Stacy: Well, you have lots of time. After the meeting, let's go and see Mr. Carlson.

Nick: Okay. Um, who is Mr. Carlson?

Stacy: He's our boss, the CEO.

> **Brief note**
> "Have a seat" is a polite way of asking someone to sit down.

> **Brief note**
> "Supervisor" is another word for *boss* (see part B). It is usually used for a lower boss who works closely with employees, not a CEO.

> **Brief note**
> A *business* is a place that sells things. *Business* is also the activity of making and selling things, and it is a university subject.

B Vocabulary

Read the conversation again. Match the expressions to the correct definitions.

1. coworker •
2. company •
3. intern •
4. employee •
5. CEO •
6. secretary •
7. boss •
8. meeting •

- • **a.** a business
- • **b.** chief executive officer; the boss of a company
- • **c.** a person whose job is to answer phones, etc.
- • **d.** a person who works at a job for a short time to learn about it
- • **e.** a person whose job is to tell others what to do
- • **f.** a time at work when people get together to discuss something
- • **g.** a person who works for another person or for a company
- • **h.** a person you work with

C Vocabulary Comprehension

Read Nick's email to his parents about his first day at work. Circle the correct answers.

Hi, Mom and Dad.

My first day at the ❶ (company / employee) is going fine. I don't have a computer yet, so I'm borrowing a tablet from the ❷ (meeting / secretary). His name is Tony. A ❸ (secretary / coworker) named Tammy introduced me to the other ❹ (companies / employees) in the office. She seems very nice. So does Stacy, my ❺ (intern / supervisor).

We just had a ❻ (boss / meeting) about this week's work. Soon Stacy is taking me to meet the big ❼ (boss / employee)—the CEO! I'm a little nervous. More later.

Love,
Nick

D Grammar

be in wh- questions; demonstratives; possessive adjectives

be in wh- questions
Wh- word + *be* + S (+ more information)
Where am I right now, and **where am** I going? **What are** you guys studying? **Who is** that woman? **When are** those meetings? **Why is** this so hard?

possessive adjectives	
singular	plural
my coworker **your** office **his** parents **her** brothers **its** CEO	**our** boss **your** company **their** supervisor

Brief note

Remember, demonstratives (*this, that, these,* and *those*) can come before a noun, or they can be alone.

Brief note

Possessives say who has something.
- You can also use a noun to talk about who has something. Add - 's to a singular noun or -s' to a plural one: *Erik's potatoes* (one person has potatoes); *the boys' room* (many boys live in a room).
- Use the question word *whose* to ask about who has something: *Whose dog is that?*

E Grammar Practice

Circle the correct answers.

1. What's (your / our) name?

2. (Who's / Whose) phone is this?

3. (Where / Here) do you live?

4. (When / Who) is your daughter's birthday?

5. The students have (there / their) pencils.

6. Is (this / these) the (boy's / boys') bathroom?

7. I enjoyed meeting (my / mine) new coworkers yesterday.

8. (This / These) math problems are more difficult than (this / those) problems.

9. (This / That) book in my hand costs more than (this / that) one over there.

10. (Where / What) is the name of (your / your's) family's company?

11. (Whose / Who) is your boss? (When / What) time is he arriving?

12. (Marks' / Mark's) keys aren't here. (Where / When) are they?

F Write to Speak

Find a partner. Ask questions about your partner and write the answers.

_____

_____

_____

_____

_____

_____

_____

G Use the Language

This is my partner...

Find another pair of partners. Introduce your partner to them. Then walk around the room and introduce your partner to at least three other pairs of partners.

Lesson 4 — Jobs

Brief note

Use *This is...* to introduce someone informally. In more formal conversations (with a boss, professor, etc.), people often use these phrases:
I'd like to introduce you to...
I'd like you to meet...
Let me introduce...

A Model Conversation

Read the conversation. Then listen. Track 07

Teacher: Sonia, I'd like to introduce you to Mr. Peters. He's our **career counselor**. Mr. Peters, this is Sonia. She wants some **advice**. She's choosing her classes for next **semester**.

Mr. Peters: Hi, Sonia. So what do you want to do after you graduate?

Sonia: Well, I'd like to be a pop star, but I can't sing. Anyway, I like clothes, and I love drawing. Maybe I want to be a fashion designer. Of course, I also like money. Maybe I want to be a CEO.

Mr. Peters: So art, design, and business could be good classes for you. Let's look at the schedule.

Brief note

Pop, as in *pop music* or *pop star*, is short for *popular*. Something popular is something a lot of people like.

B Vocabulary

Match the words under the pictures to the correct definitions.

a. graduate

b. draw

c. pop star

d. clothes

e. creative

f. fashion designer

_____ having many new ideas

_____ a popular singer

_____ a person who makes clothes

_____ things to wear

_____ to finish school or college

_____ to make a picture

Look back at the conversation in part A. Write the bold words next to the correct definitions.

1. _____ an opinion told to someone about what he or she should do

2. _____ a job that someone does for a long time; a person's work life

3. _____ a person whose job is to listen and give advice

4. _____ half of a school or university year, often eighteen weeks

C In Your World

Fill in the blanks. Then read your answers to your classmates and listen to their answers.

I want to take a(n) _____ class.

I want to be a(n) _____.

D Grammar

want (to) and *would like (to)*

Brief note

Sometimes *want* and *would like* can be used in the same place. At those times, *would like* is more formal than *want*.

want / would like + noun	*want to / would like to* + verb
Would like + noun is a less direct, more polite way of saying that you want something.	*Would like to* means *want to*. It is less direct, so it can also be used for wishes that cannot happen.
I **want** a pizza. / I **would like** a pizza. I **want** some new clothes. / I **would like** some new clothes.	I **want to** become a fashion designer. I **would like** to become a fashion designer. I **would like** to be a pop star (but I can't sing).
To make short forms with *would like*, add *-'d* to the subject pronoun: *I'd, you'd, he'd, she'd, it'd, we'd, they'd.* I**'d like** to see a career counselor. She**'d like** dessert. We**'d like** to graduate this year.	

E Grammar Practice

Put the words in order to make sentences.

1. like / you / would / or / coffee / tea

   _____?

2. lawyer / a / be / to / like / he'd

   _____.

3. do / you / what / like / would / to

   _____?

4. class / want / a / business / they / good

   _____.

5. go / like / moon / to / I'd / the / to

   _____.

F Listen to Speak

Read the information. Then listen to the introductions. Write the name of the person in each picture. Track 08

He's married and has a son. He loves his job and likes to give advice to students. In the summer, he travels with his family. He'd like to go to Mt. Everest, but he's too busy.	She's married, with no kids. She studies computer science in college and also works at a big company. She wants to be a CEO someday.	She's single and lives with her best friend. They're creative and love the arts. She's a part-time barista now, but she would like to be a movie star.
_____	_____	_____

1. Interview a partner about a person he or she knows (not a classmate).
2. Tell your classmates about the person, and answer any questions they have.

A Model Monologues

Read the monologues. Write the number of each monologue next to the correct picture. Then listen. Track 09

1. **Man:** I'm from San Francisco. It's an urban area in the state of California. There's a very famous bridge there, the Golden Gate Bridge. San Francisco is beside a bay. There are tall buildings, and some mountains are nearby. I love my hometown.

2. **Woman:** I'm from Helena, Montana. It's small, but it's a beautiful town. It's very rural. It usually snows a lot in the winter, but the summer is very hot. It's an awesome place.

3. **Man:** My hometown is Nashville, Tennessee. People call it "Music City." You can hear all kinds of music every night, but country music is the most popular. Nashville is also famous for great food, and the people are really nice.

B Vocabulary

Read the monologues again. Write the words from the box under the correct pictures.

| bridge | urban | bay | rural | mountain |

1. _____ 2. _____ 3. _____ 4. _____

Match the words to the correct definitions.

6. famous   • a. very pretty
7. hometown   • b. a part of a larger place
8. beautiful   • c. known to very many people
9. area   • d. the city or town where a person is from
10. state   • e. a part of a country that can make some of its own laws

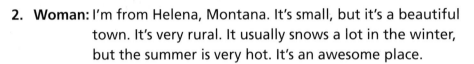

5. _____

C In Your World

Use a dictionary. Find five English adjectives that describe your hometown. Write them here.

1. _____ 2. _____ 3. _____ 4. _____ 5. _____

D Grammar

Questions with *be like*; adjectives

Brief note

Go back to p. 11 to review S + *be* + adj. See p. 73 to learn about adjectives after other verbs.

questions with *be like*	adjectives	
These questions ask you to describe a person or place.	You can describe things using adjectives. Adjectives can come after some verbs or before nouns.	
***What* + *be* + S + *like* (+ more information)?**	**S + V + adj.**	**(article +) adj. + N**
What **is** he **like**? What**'s** Paris **like** at night? Who's your favorite professor? What**'s** she **like**? What **are** your parents **like** when they're angry?	He's **calm** and **quiet**. It's **beautiful** and **exciting**. She's **loud** and **passionate**.	a **quiet** man **beautiful** lights She's a **passionate** person.

E Grammar Practice

Brief note

Remember to use *a* before words that begin with a consonant sound and *an* before words that begin with a vowel sound.

Put the words in order to make sentences.

1. mother / is / what / your / like _____ ?
2. your / like / siblings / are / what _____ ?
3. blue / Marcia / a / has / car _____ .
4. in / house / an / boy / lives / tall / the / old _____ .
5. beautiful / famous / she's / and _____ .

F Read to Write

Read the advertisement. Underline the adjectives. Look up any words you don't know.

Want to visit an exciting place? Come to Australia!

Whatever you'd like to do, you can do it here. There are big cities with beautiful beaches and great seafood restaurants. Australia is famous for its awesome weather. It's usually hot and sunny, even in winter. You can swim in the ocean all year.

Would you like to leave the crowded city and relax in the country? The huge rural part of Australia is called the Outback. You can go there to see amazing animals, like kangaroos.

Come and see what Australia is like!

G Use the Language

Travel to my hometown.

What's your hometown like? Why would travelers like to go there? Write a paragraph about it. Look back at part C for ideas.

My hometown: _____

Listen to a conversation between a reporter for the school newspaper and a college soccer player. Fill in the blanks with the words that you hear. Track 10

Jamie: Excuse me. _____ you Daniel Bell?

Daniel: Yes, I _____. Hello. Are you the reporter?

Jamie: Yes. Jamie White, from the university newspaper. Nice to _____ you.

Daniel: Nice to meet you, too. Have a _____.

Jamie: Thanks. By the _____, congratulations on _____ the big game!

Daniel: Thanks. Yeah, it feels good to win.

Jamie: In the story, I'm going to _____ you to our readers. So first, _____ are you from?

Daniel: A small town in the _____ of Washington, near Seattle.

Jamie: How _____ life there?

Daniel: _____. It's a beautiful area.

Jamie: _____ your family there?

Daniel: Yes, they _____. I have two brothers there. They love soccer, too.

Jamie: So, what about your career, if you don't _____ my asking? Would you like to be a _____ soccer player?

Daniel: No, actually. I want to be a _____, like you.

With a partner, think of a famous person that you both know a lot about. Use the Internet for ideas. Then decide on roles. One of you is that person, and the other is a reporter interviewing him or her. Role-play the interview. Try to include the following:

- Introductions
- Where the person is from
- Basic details about the person's family and career
- What the person wants to do in the future

Some Module 1 Goals in Unit 1

Put a check mark (✓) next to the things you can do.

_____ Understand and use words and phrases about family, personal details, and simple everyday situations

_____ Communicate information about yourself, your family, your job, and where you come from in a simple and direct exchange

_____ Build a basic vocabulary of words and phrases to talk about yourself and communicate in common everyday situations

Read to Write

Read the letter from your new pen friend.

Hello,

How are you? Let me introduce myself. My name is Anaya, and I live in
Vancouver, Canada. I'm 20 years old, and I go to the University of Art
and Design. The campus is beautiful. I like urban life! It's new for me
because I'm from a rural area in India. My parents and my brother live there.
I study web design, the designing of websites. I'm creative, and I love computers. Someday,
I'd like to own a web design company. My classes are hard, but I like them. I study a lot, but
I also have fun with my friends. Vancouver is amazing.

What about you? Are you a student? What's your hometown like? What's your future
career? Is your family big? Sorry—that's a lot of questions! By the way, I'm sending a photo.
Can you please send me one, too?

Anaya

Prewrite

Get ready to write to Anaya. Use the letter to fill in Anaya's answers to the questions, and then fill in your answers. Think of two more questions you'd like to ask her.

	Anaya	You
How old are you?		
Where are you from?		
What are you like?		
What's your future career?		

Now Write

Respond to Anaya's letter. Introduce yourself, answer her questions, and ask your questions. Start here and, if necessary, continue on a separate piece of paper.

A Model Conversation

Read the conversation. Then listen. Track 11

Brief note
We say "huh" in a statement when something is interesting. We ask *huh?* as a question when we want someone to repeat. As a question, *huh* is very informal.

Jim: So, what do you think of this weather?

Terry: I hate it. It's so hot here in the summer! I don't like high temperatures.

Jim: Oh. Huh. I'm from Arizona. This feels quite cool to me.

Terry: Then you won't like winter here. There's a lot of snow. And it's really cold, sometimes five degrees below zero.

Jim: Below zero? In Celsius or Fahrenheit?

Terry: Celsius.

Jim: That's not too bad. Anyway, in the winter, I'm going back to my hometown. It's such a great place.

Terry: What's the weather like there?

Jim: It's usually sunny and clear. It's hot and dry, never humid. By the way, how's the weather here in spring and fall?

Terry: It's great—cool and sunny. Those are the best seasons.

Brief note
In weather forecasts, "C" stands for Celsius. "F" stands for Fahrenheit. In the US, people usually use Fahrenheit. People in other English-speaking countries usually use Celsius.

B Vocabulary

Match the words under the pictures to the correct definitions.

a. temperature

b. dry

c. season

_____ what it's like outside: hot, cold, rainy, etc.

_____ spring, summer, fall, or winter

_____ an opinion about how the weather will be

_____ how hot or cold it is

_____ not rainy or wet

_____ not cloudy; sunny

d. forecast

e. clear

f. weather

Circle the correct answers.

1. The temperature is high. The weather is _____. a. cold   b. hot   c. rainy
2. The temperature is low. The weather is _____. a. cold   b. hot   c. rainy
3. We use degrees to measure _____. a. height   b. rain   c. temperatures
4. It's cloudy. The weather is NOT _____. a. dry   b. sunny   c. hot
5. It's humid. The weather is NOT _____. a. dry   b. sunny   c. hot

C In Your World

Work with a partner. Describe the weather. What's it like today? What's it usually like in each of the four seasons?

Grammar

Simple present questions with *what* and *how*; intensifiers

What/How + V + S (+ more information)?	answers
How are you? **How** does Alicia like the cake? **What**'s the weather like? **What** does Chris do? **What** do you think of this weather?	I'm great. She says it's delicious! It's sunny and dry. He's a teacher. I don't like it. / It's too hot. / I think it's amazing!

What do you think of...? and ***How do you like...?*** are both invitations to tell your opinion.
How about + **noun**? can be used in informal English to ask for an opinion:
    How about *this weather?*   ***How about*** *that game?*
In answers, remember to add an *-s* for third person singular subjects:
    She really likes it.	

intensifiers: *so, quite, really, such*	
S + *be* + intensifier + adj.	**S + *be* + *such* (+ article) (+ adj.) + noun**
It's **really** hot. She's **so** cold! We're **quite** good.	It's **such** an old song. They're **such** bad students. You're **such** a good cook.

Grammar Practice

Circle the correct answers.

1. (How's / What's) Josh?

2. (How's / What's) Josh like?

3. (What do you think / How do you like) of this school?

4. (What do you think / How do you like) your cake?

5. He's (so / such) fast!

6. It's (such a / so) big dog!

7. Roberto is (quite / quite a) tired.

8. What (do / are) they like to eat?

9. (What's / What) your name?

10. (How / How are) you feeling?

11. You're (such / such a) good teacher.

12. That's (such a / such) great story.

Use the Language

Weather forecasts

1. Find a local weather forecast for the next week. Discuss the forecast with a partner.

2. Write a paragraph about the weather for the next week. Read your paragraph to your partner.

A Model Conversation

Read the conversation. Then listen. 🎧 Track 12

Tori: So, do you have a job?

Luke: Yeah, I do. I'm a part-time mechanic. I work on weekends.

Tori: Oh, cool. Are you a part-time student, too?

Luke: No, I'm full-time. How about you? What do you do?

Tori: I'm a full-time student too, but I have a part-time job in the library. My parents pay my tuition, but I help with money from my job.

Luke: That's nice. What's your major?

Tori: I'm majoring in computer engineering.

Luke: And what do you want to do after you graduate?

Tori: I'd like to design software. What about you?

Luke: I want to be an architect. I'm also minoring in English literature.

Tori: Interesting. Why did you choose literature?

Luke: I just love to read.

> **Brief note**
> The word "software" means the programs that run on a computer.

B Vocabulary

Listen to the conversation again. Match the words to the correct definitions. 🎧 Track 12

1. part-time
2. engineering
3. choose
4. mechanic
5. full-time
6. minor
7. architect
8. major
9. tuition

a. a person who fixes cars
b. a student's main study subject
c. a person who designs buildings
d. all the time; all day, every workday
e. some of the time; a few hours a day
f. the money that students pay for classes
g. a student's second main study subject
h. to pick; to decide between several choices
i. the study and design of things people make, like bridges, cars, computers, etc.

C Vocabulary Comprehension

Read the email. Fill in the blanks with the correct words from the box.

part-time	minor	engineering	major	tuition	architect

Dear Mr. Watkins,

My name is Nathan Ray. I'm a freshman, and I'm trying to choose a(n) ❶ _____ . I think I'd like to be a(n) ❷ _____ like my dad. He designed the school library. But I also really like my grandfather's job. He helped design the Golden Gate Bridge. So should I also major in ❸ _____ ? Or should it be my ❹ _____ ?

Can we please meet soon? I have a(n) ❺ _____ job in the cafeteria three days a week to help pay my ❻ _____ . But I have free time on Tuesdays and Thursdays.

Sincerely,
Nathan

D In Your World

Ask three of your classmates if they have jobs, and fill in the chart. Ask follow-up questions and make notes about the answers. Then share your chart with the class.

Name	Job? (If yes, what job?)	Part-time (P/T) or full-time (F/T)?	Notes
1.	Yes / No (_____)		
2.	Yes / No (_____)		
3.	Yes / No (_____)		

E Grammar

Simple present yes/no questions; objects

> **Brief note**
> These answers can all be shortened to *Yes, + S + do(es)* or *No, + S + do(es)n't.*

yes/no questions	answers
***Do(es)* + S + V (+ more information)?**	***Yes/No,* + S + *do(es)* (+ *not*) + V (+ more information).**
Do you **like** (hot dogs)? object	No, I **don't like** hot dogs.
Do you **have** (a job)? object	Yes, I **have** a job.
Does it **work**?	No, it **doesn't**.
Does he **have** money?	Yes, he **has** money.
Do you **have** a dog?	No, I **don't have** one.
Do they **have** a son?	No, they **don't have** one.

> **Brief note**
> Some verbs have objects and others don't. *Have* always needs an object.

> **Brief note**
> A person isn't counting when they use *one* in an object position. It's used to replace the noun—the object. For example:
> Q: *Do you have a job?*
> A: *Yes, I have one.*
> Here, *one* is a job.

Look at the table above. Circle all of the objects.

F Grammar Practice

Fill in the blanks with correct answers.

1. Do you have a pencil?   Yes, _____. / No, _____.
2. Do you take taxis?   Yes, _____. / No, _____.
3. Does he have a brother? Yes, _____. / No, _____.
4. Do you want dessert?   Yes, _____. / No, _____.
5. Does she have a dog?   Yes, _____. / No, _____.

Put the words in order to make questions.

6. you / a / job / full-time / do / have   _____?
7. Josie / does / engineering / study   _____?
8. work / they / do / weekends / on   _____?

G Use the Language

Class party

When people meet for the first time, they usually introduce themselves and then make small talk. Topics can include **weather, jobs/school, family,** and **hobbies** (things you like to do).

Stand up. Imagine you are at a party. You don't know anyone. Mingle—move around and talk to people. Make small talk with at least three people. Try to speak to each person about all of the topics above, and to remember what you hear. Then report to the class.

A — Model Conversation

Read the conversation. Then listen. 🔘 Track 13

Brief note

An "only child" is a person with no siblings.

Juan: Okay. I should get going. Talk to you later. Sorry, that was my little brother.

Nikki: Really? I thought you were an only child! How many siblings do you have?

Juan: Two little brothers. The younger one, Rafael, is so funny. When I'm with him, I laugh a lot. But Javi is the opposite—he's tall and thin. He's quite serious, and very intelligent.

Nikki: Huh. So, how about your parents?

Juan: My mother is such a friendly person. Everyone loves her. My dad's shy, but he's really funny, too. Anyway, so now you know everything about me. What about you? Do you have any siblings?

Brief note

"Opposite" means *completely different*. For example, the opposite of *tall* is *short*. The opposite of *funny* is *serious*.

B — Vocabulary

Read the conversation again. Then fill in the blanks with the correct forms of the words.

sibling

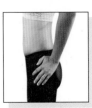
fat

thin

friendly

shy

serious

intelligent

smile

laugh

1. Don't be _____! Say hello and introduce yourself.
2. A: Why are you _____ so loud? B: We're watching a funny movie.
3. Michelle is the most _____ person in this class. She always gets As.
4. Jesse is such a happy and friendly person. He _____ all the time.
5. I have three _____—two sisters and a brother.
6. Stephen doesn't eat very much. He's too _____.

C — About You

Choose two members of your family. Write two adjectives to describe each of them. Don't use the same adjective twice.

Person 1: Who? _____   What is he or she like? _____ _____

Person 2: Who? _____   What is he or she like? _____ _____

Now practice describing each family member to a partner.

D Grammar

Questions with *any* and *how many*; object pronouns

Do you have *any* pens?

Yes, I do.

How many pens do you have?

Only one.

Oh. Well, can I borrow *it* for a second?

Sometimes, *any* goes before a noun. It means *more than zero, nothing,* or *none.* Answer an *any* question with *yes* or *no.*

In questions, *how many* goes before a noun. Answer a *how many* question with a number.

After a verb, *it* is an object pronoun. In this conversation, *it* means the one pen.

Object pronouns: *me, you, him, her, it, us, them*	Use an object pronoun only when the listener or reader knows the main noun.
You know **me.** Do you trust **me**?	The listener knows *me*—*me* is the person talking.
He likes **that book.** Can he have **it**?	The listener knows *it* is *that book*—the speaker says *that book* in the previous sentence.
Is that **Jim**? Give **him** the key.	The listener knows that *him* means *Jim*—the speaker mentions Jim in the previous sentence.
Clara! There's a phone call for **you**.	Clara knows that *you* means *Clara*—the speaker calls her name before saying *you*.

E Grammar Practice

Fill in the blanks with the correct words. Then write answers that are true for you.

1. Q: Do you have _____ more classes today?   A: _____.

2. Q: _____ _____ uncles do you have?   A: _____.

3. Q: Do you have _____ cousins?   A: _____.

Put the words in order to make pairs of sentences.

4. find / I / phone / can't / my   you / it / Do / see

    _____.   _____?

5. are / Your / here / friends   in / them / Let

    _____.   _____.

6. Anita's / umbrella / That's   it / her / to / Give

    _____.   _____.

7. here, / Antonio / Come   money / have / for / I / some / you

    _____.   _____.

F Use the Language

A descriptive paragraph

Choose any friend, family member, or famous person. On a separate piece of paper, write a description of him or her. Then share your description with the class.

Lesson 4 — I study English because...

A   Model Monologue

Read the monologue. Then listen. 🎧 Track 14

Ted: Some people study English to get a good job. English is the international language of business, and pilots from all countries use it, too. Other people study English because they want to attend an American university or move to the United States or another English-speaking country. Others are curious. They want to learn English so they can talk with foreigners and learn about their countries. I study English for a different reason. I study because I set a goal to speak seven languages, and English is my third one. I also know Spanish and French. Sometimes English is difficult. But remember why you're studying it. Thinking about your goal will help you.

B   Vocabulary

Study the monologue again. Then match the expressions to the correct definitions.

> **a.** move   **b.** set a goal   **c.** talk with   **d.** attend
> **e.** difficult   **f.** foreigner   **g.** pilot   **h.** international   **i.** curious

_____ an airplane's driver   _____ to speak to   _____ to decide to do something

_____ to change houses   _____ very hard   _____ a person from another country

_____ want to know   _____ to go to   _____ related to more than one country

C   Vocabulary Comprehension

Brief note

A *goal* is something good that you want and plan to do. To decide to do it is to *set* a goal, and to do it is to *reach* your goal. Here, *reach* means *do* or *finish*.

Listen to the woman. Fill in the blanks. 🎧 Track 15

1. The woman says people should learn to _____ _____.

2. She says a good goal is _____ but is something you can do.

3. The woman wants to _____ to America and _____ college there.

4. She wants to major in _____ _____.

5. She needs to _____ _____ people from other countries.

D   About You

What is your biggest goal for this week? Write it below. Then talk about it with a partner.

My goal for this week is to _____

_____.

26

Grammar

Questions with *why*; conjunction *because*; infinitives of purpose

questions with *why*	*because*	infinitives
Why asks for a reason.	You can use *because* + S + V to give a reason. Use it before or after another S + V. In speaking, it can be alone.	infinitive = *to* + verb. Sometimes an infinitive gives a goal or a reason for doing something.
Why is she learning Chinese? **Why** are his eyes closed? **Why** does Andre study? **Why** do you exercise?	**Because** she wants to live in China. His eyes are closed **because** he wants to sleep. **Because** he wants to get good grades, he always studies hard. I exercise **because** I want to be healthy.	She likes **to study** Chinese. (object of the verb) He studies **to get good grades**. (reason for studying) I exercise **to be healthy**. (reason for exercising)

Brief note

With infinitives of purpose, you can usually add *in order* in front of *to*: *I exercise in order to be healthy.*

Grammar Practice

Combine the sentences to make one sentence. Use *because* or an infinitive.

1. Oscar walks to school. He wants to save money.

   _____.

2. Jenna is going to medical school. She wants to be a doctor.

   _____.

3. I don't like seafood. It makes me feel sick.

   _____.

Write *why* questions for these answers.

4. I like Brenda because she's friendly.

   _____?

5. Manny watches English movies and TV shows to improve his listening.

   _____?

6. They're going to a café because they're very hungry.

   _____?

Use the Language

Why study English?

Work in groups. Think of five reasons to study English. Make a list and share it with your class. Then listen to other groups' reasons. Write down your five favorite reasons from other groups.

Your group's reasons:	**Other groups' reasons:**
_____	_____
_____	_____
_____	_____
_____	_____
_____	_____

A Model Conversation

Brief note
Here, "big" means important.

Read the conversation. Then listen. 🎧 Track 16

Belinda: Are you coming to the baseball game with us?

Carlos: I'd like to, but I can't.

Belinda: Why not? It's a big game. The **winners** are **league champions**.

Carlos: I've got to study for my algebra test.

Belinda: A test? That doesn't sound so important. You should come.

Carlos: I've got to get an A on this test. It's **half** my grade.

Belinda: Yeah, you have to study, then. Too bad. The team needs fans there to cheer.

Carlos: I've got to do laundry, too, or I won't have any clean clothes to wear tomorrow.

Belinda: You're going to be busy. Well, have fun. I have to get going. I don't want to **miss** the first pitch.

Carlos: I have to run too. Catch you later.

B Vocabulary

Read the conversation again. Look at the bold words. Write them next to the correct definitions.

1. _____ 50%; ½
2. _____ to not see something because you weren't there; to not be able to attend
3. _____ the people or team who wins
4. _____ a group of sports teams that play each other
5. _____ the best team in a league

Write the words from the box under the correct pictures.

algebra
grade
pitch
cheer

6. _____   7. _____   8. _____   9. _____

C Vocabulary: Ending a conversation

Study the informal ways of ending a conversation. Then read the conversations and fill in the blanks. Listen and check. 🎧 Track 17

I have to get going.	Catch you later.	Have fun!	I have to run.

1. **Tanya:** Wow, it's 4:00! I _____ _____ run.

   Cam: Yeah, I have to _____ _____, too. See you later!

2. **Tanya:** I'm meeting a friend for dinner soon. I'll see you tomorrow.

   Cam: Okay, _____ _____!

   Tanya: Thanks. _____ _____ _____.

D Grammar

should and *have (got) to*

should/shouldn't + base verb	
Should + verb is used to give advice or suggestions. It means something is a good idea. *should not = shouldn't*	You look sick. You **should** see a doctor. She **shouldn't** watch TV tonight. She **should** study for her test.
have to and *have got to*	
Have to + verb and *have got to* + verb mean *need to*. These expressions are stronger than *should*. They mean something is necessary.	I **have to** use the restroom. I **have got to** go to the bathroom.
In *have got to*, the short form of *have* is often used: I / you / we / they + *have* = *I've, you've, we've, they've* He / she / (name) + *has* = *He's, she's, (name)'s*	You**'ve got to** eat. We**'ve got to** clean. He**'s got to** work. She**'s got to** study. Paul**'s got to** get going. Tamara**'s got to** move.

> **Brief note**
>
> In speaking, *got to* is often pronounced "gotta." Informally, with subjects that are not third person singular, *have* is sometimes not used—for example, *I gotta go.* 🔘 Track 18

E Grammar Practice

Circle the correct answers.

1. Laura (has to / should) wake up early for school. She (has to / should) go to bed at 10:00.

2. (Pedro / Pedro's) has to go to an important meeting. He (should / shouldn't) wear nice clothes.

3. Manuel (should / shouldn't) walk home. It's late. He (has to / should) take a taxi.

4. I (should / have got to) go to bed, but I can't. (I've / I) got to watch my favorite soccer team.

F Quick Review

Look back at the brief notes in this module. What word or phrase can you use to...

1. ...begin a conversation? _____

2. ...informally ask someone to repeat something? _____

3. ...politely begin or end a personal question? _____

4. ...tell someone to sit down? _____

G Use the Language

Advice, please.

Work in pairs. One partner is a student, and the other is a student counselor. Read the information below.

- **Student**: You're taking a lot of classes, and you also have a part-time job. You never have any free time. You'd like to quit your job, but you want the money because you want to buy a car.

- **Counselor**: Your job is to listen to the student's problems and give advice.

Think about what you want to say. Then role-play the conversation.

Switch roles. After practicing, perform your conversation for the class.

Advice in an Email

Hi, Carlos.

How are you? We're good. The weather here is hot and sunny right now, but the forecast says the weekend will be humid and rainy. How's the weather there? What do you think of your new professors?

I'm sorry to hear you're not feeling well. Do you stay up late every night? You've got to get more sleep. You have to take care of yourself, son! I'd like to come and see you this weekend, but I can't because I have to take my car to the mechanic.

Do you ever see Nick, from high school, on campus? He's such a nice, intelligent guy. You should get together with him.

Your sister is really curious about how you're doing. You should call her. She, your dad, and I are all fine.

Love,
Mom

List the advice in the email under the correct expressions.

should	have to / have got to

B **Give Advice**

Pretend you have a friend or family member who is deciding on a major. This person is interested in both English and engineering and asks you for advice. Write an email giving your advice.

_____

_____

_____

_____

_____

C **Reminder**

Some Module 1 Goals in Unit 2

Put a check mark (✓) next to the things you can do.

_____ Describe your family simply (for example, who the members are, how old they are, and what they do)

_____ Write simply about simple topics, such as the weather

_____ Join phrases with words like *and* or *because*

A Warm Up

In part B, a student describes his family. Look at the picture below and put a check mark (✓) next to the words you think he's going to use. Then write two more words you think he could use.

☐ smile   ☐ siblings   ☐ friendly   ☐ _____

☐ sunny   ☐ engineer   ☐ serious   ☐ _____

☐ fat   ☐ difficult   ☐ beautiful

B Listen for Information

Listen to Mateo describe himself and his family. Then answer the questions. 🎧 Track 19

1. What's the weather like in Mateo's hometown?
   _____

2. How many of Mateo's siblings are friendly?
   _____

3. Who is shy? _____

4. Which family member is funny? _____

5. Which one is serious? _____

6. What should Mateo do? _____

C "Find someone who…"

Question your classmates until you find someone for every item on this list.

Find someone who…

❶ …does not have any siblings.

❷ …has five people in their family.

❸ …is studying English to get a good job.

❹ …has a job.

❺ …is feeling great.

❻ …comes from a sunny place.

❼ …really likes snow.

❽ …has to wake up early.

Name

❶ _____

❷ _____

❸ _____

❹ _____

❺ _____

❻ _____

❼ _____

❽ _____

D Write

Write a paragraph about your list on a separate piece of paper. Then share your paragraph with a partner. Do you have similar information?

A Vocabulary

Remember and write…

1. …five jobs.

    _____ _____ _____ _____ _____

2. …four ways to end a conversation.

    _____ _____ _____ _____

3. …four adjectives to describe a place.

    _____ _____ _____ _____

4. …three adjectives to describe weather.

    _____ _____ _____

5. …four adjectives to describe a person.

    _____ _____ _____ _____

6. …two ways to introduce someone. Then flip through the module, if necessary, and write one more.

    _____ _____ _____

B Grammar

Look back at the module. Fill in the blanks.

1. Are _____ an architect?

2. He's _____ a teacher. He's a student.

3. How _____ is it to the store?

4. What time is _____?

5. Who _____ I?

6. _____ are you late for class?

7. Give Jim's pencil back to _____, please.

8. _____ you like a cup of tea?

9. A: Does she have a sweater?

    B: Yes, she has _____.

10. What do you _____ of my new car?

11. You have _____ a beautiful home!

12. Do you have _____ ice cream?

13. _____ _____ jobs do you have?

14. Here, Roberto, I'm giving my pie to _____.

15. I want _____ move to Australia.

16. Jaime is going to bed _____ he is tired.

17. Mom says I've _____ _____ be home by 11 p.m.

18. We _____ to go now.

C Practicing Small Talk

Review the model conversations in Units 1 and 2. With a partner, practice having several short conversations about the following topics:

| the weather today | sports | your hometown | your classes and grades |

Take turns starting and ending the conversations.

To start: *What do you think of...?*   *What do you do?*   *How are you doing?*

To end: *I've got to be going.*   *Catch you later.*   *Bye.*

D Introduce the Team

Form groups of four to six students. You all work together at the same company. Think of a job title and two adjectives for each group member. Write a description of your new "team," and then practice introducing yourself and your team to other teams in the class.

My name is...   I...   And let me introduce...   He's our...

This is my...   Her name is...   She's intelligent and...

E The Man in the Photo

Write five questions about the man in the photo. Then ask and answer the questions with a partner.

Name: Gabriel Rodriguez

Job: engineer

Lives in: Guadalajara

Siblings: sister, brother

Father: architect

Mother: teacher

Likes: listening to music, exercising

Is: thin, friendly, quiet, intelligent

1. _____
2. _____
3. _____
4. _____
5. _____

Now, on a separate sheet of paper, write a paragraph (at least five sentences) introducing the man. Use the information above and your own ideas.

You're a student.

Module 2 Goals

Build a very basic vocabulary of words and phrases about personal details and simple everyday situations
Very simply describe where you go to school
Ask and answer simple questions and respond to simple statements on very familiar topics (for example, student life) with help
Describe what you like and don't like (for example, with regard to school)
Understand people if they speak very slowly and clearly about simple everyday topics
Find basic information in posters or advertisements
Describe your education
Complete a questionnaire with information about your educational background

Preview

Look at pages 36 to 61. What pages are these things on?

two men boxing   _____

a lot of money   _____

a woman on a horse   _____

a questionnaire with boxes for checks   _____

Write and Discuss

Write your answers to the questions. Then talk about them with a partner.

1. Where do you go to school?
   I go to …

2. What do you like about your home? What don't you like?
   I like …
   I don't like …

3. What do you study now? What's your major?

4. What are some things you can find on a school campus?

5. Who are some famous people, and what do they do?

Unit 3

Unit 4

Scan the QR code to watch a preview video.

★ Unit 3 · Your University ★

Lesson 1 — I'm a student.

A Model Conversation

Read the conversation. Then listen. 🔘 Track 20

> **Brief note**
>
> *What are you doing?* asks about your actions right now. "What do you do?" asks about your job.

Alex: Iris, let me introduce you to my cousin Kevin.
Iris: Hi, Kevin. It's nice to meet you. So, what do you do?
Kevin: I'm a college student. I start classes next week.
Iris: Oh, that's cool. I'm a student too. I attend UNM in Santa Fe. Where do you go?
Kevin: I go to Saint John's College. It's also in Santa Fe.
Iris: Aha. Alex, you're a Saint John's graduate, right?
Alex: Yeah, that's right. Class of 2009.
Iris: And how old are you, Kevin?
Kevin: I'm 18. I'm starting my first semester in college.
Iris: So you're a freshman. I remember those days. I'm a senior. I graduate next spring.
Kevin: What do you want to do after you graduate?
Iris: I'm getting a degree in computer science. I want to be a computer engineer.

B Vocabulary: The US school system

American School System—Primary and Secondary		College/University Years	
primary/elementary school	= the first years of school for children	first year	= freshman
secondary school	= middle school + high school	second year	= sophomore
middle school	= the years between primary school and high school	third year	= junior
high school	= the last years of secondary school	fourth year	= senior

Match the words from the box to the correct definitions.

1. _____ to attend
2. _____ a person working in engineering
3. _____ a way to say the year you graduated
4. _____ a title given to someone for finishing a college program (for example, BA, BS, PhD)
5. _____ a person who has a degree from a school or college program

a. go to
b. degree
c. class of...
d. engineer
e. graduate/grad

C Pronunciation

Study the pronunciations and definitions of *graduate*. Practice saying each word. Which one sounds different?

> **graduate¹** /ɡræ'ju et/ *verb* to finish a school or college program
> **graduate²** /ɡræ'ju ət/ *noun* a person who has a degree from a school or college
> **graduate³** /ɡræ'ju ət/ *adjective* used before a noun to describe studying for a higher degree (after a BA/BS)

Write *verb*, *noun*, or *adjective* under the underlined words. Then listen and repeat. 🔘 Track 21

1. He's a college <u>graduate</u>.   2. I'm a <u>graduate</u> student.   3. We'll <u>graduate</u> in June.

Grammar

Brief note

Simple present of *do* and *go*

Occupation means *job* or *career*.

do	*go*
I **do**	I **go**
He / She / It **does**	He / She / It **goes**
We / You / They **do**	We / You / They **go**

Brief note

In questions like *What does he do?* and *Where does she go?* the first *do* agrees with the subject.

useful expressions		
To talk about someone's occupation (reporter, student, secretary, etc.)	A: What **does** he **do**? A: What **do** you **do**?	B: He **is** a doctor. B: I **work** for a newspaper. **I am** a reporter.
To talk about which school someone attends and what someone studies	A: Where **does** she **go**? A: What **do** you **study**?	B: She **goes** to Oklahoma State University. B: I **study** music **at** Barton College.

E **Grammar Practice**

Circle the correct answers.

1. What (do / are) his parents do?

2. Eleanor (does / is) an engineer.

3. My brother (works / does) at a hospital.

4. Where does Jeff (goes / go)?

5. What (do / does) they study?

6. She (goes / go) to a small college.

Fill in the blanks to complete the conversations.

7. Q: Nice to meet you. What _____ you _____?
   A: I _____ a police officer.

8. Q: What _____ your sister _____?
   A: She _____ a graduate student at Cornell.

9. Q: Which college _____ Bernard _____ to?
   A: He _____ to UCLA.

10. Q: Which medical school _____ they _____ to?
    A: They _____ to Harvard Medical School.

F **Use the Language**

What do they do?

Write the name of the job under each picture. (Look up any jobs you don't know.) Then talk with a partner about the jobs. What do you have to do before you can get these jobs?

_____ _____ _____ _____

_____ _____ _____ _____

A Model Conversation

Read the conversation. Then listen. 🎧 Track 22

Jenny: Hey, Owen. I hear you're planning to go to Simmons College in the fall. I go there too.

Owen: Oh, cool. Maybe you can show me around campus.

Jenny: Sure. What's your major?

Owen: I plan to major in geography.

Jenny: Really? That's my major.

Owen: Great! Then I have a lot of questions for you. Are you in your second year?

Jenny: No, third year. I'm a junior.

Owen: Are there many geography students?

Jenny: No, it's a small department—about fifty students. We all know each other.

Owen: Okay, good. How much homework do you have every night?

Jenny: For each class, we usually have to do a little reading and write answers to a few questions.

B Vocabulary: Some majors

Write the name of the correct major under each picture.

| fine arts | business administration | mathematics | elementary education |
| physical education | nursing | software engineering | cosmetology |

_____

_____

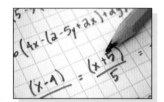

_____

_____

_____

_____

_____

_____

C Grammar

Countable and uncountable nouns

countable		uncountable	
determiners	example nouns	determiners	example nouns
a lot of many several few / a few	class**es** question**s** student**s**	a lot of (not) much little / a little	space education advice

how many and how much

how many and how much	
Use *How many...?* when asking about something countable. Use *How much...?* when asking about something uncountable.	
How many...?	**How much...?**
How many books did you buy? **How many classes** are you taking? **How many bottles** of milk do you need?	**How much money** do you have? **How much homework** do you get? **How much juice** did you drink?

Brief note

With uncountable nouns, *much* is usually only used in questions and negatives. *A lot of* is more common in affirmative statements. *Do you have much time? I don't have much money.*

D Grammar Practice

Circle the correct answers.

1. I don't have (some / many) (pencils / milk).

2. I didn't get (much / many) rest this weekend.

3. Please give me (a few / a little) bottles of juice.

4. How (much / a few) (salt / onions) did you put in the soup?

5. There's (a lot of / many) space in the living room.

6. My friend (does / doesn't) have much free time.

7. (Several / A little) people came to the theater.

8. I don't want my children to eat (a lot of / many) ice cream.

Write brief answers to the following questions. Then discuss your answers with a partner.

9. How many people live in your hometown?

_____.

10. How much homework do you have this week?

_____.

11. How much free time do you have today?

_____.

E Use the Language

Choosing a program

Which of these programs would you like to attend? Read and choose. Then discuss with a partner.

College	Degree Program	Description
Aveda Institute, New York	Two-year Cosmetology program	One of the biggest beauty schools in New York; 75% of graduates have jobs within six months.
Carnegie Mellon U., Pennsylvania	PhD in Software Engineering	Graduates work at Apple, Intel, Microsoft, Yahoo, and Adobe
Harvard University, Massachusetts	Master's in Business Administration	The number-one MBA program in the United States
University of California, Berkeley	Bachelor's Degree in Mathematics	One of the most famous math programs in the world

Sather Tower, University of California-Berkeley

Lesson 3 — Which school do you go to?

A Model Conversation

Read the conversation. Then listen. ⊙ Track 23

Olivia: What do you want to do after you graduate, José?
José: Make movies.
Olivia: You want to be a movie director?
José: Yes, that's my plan. I'm going to film school now. I'm studying for my bachelor's degree.
Olivia: Which film school do you go to?
José: Tisch School of the Arts. It's part of New York University.
Olivia: Oh, I know that school! That's Steven Spielberg's school, right?
José: No, I think he went to school in California. But Ang Lee is a graduate of my school. He's the director of *The Life of Pi*. Another famous grad is Martin Scorsese.
Olivia: That's cool. So, do you want to make films like theirs?
José: Not really. I want my movies to be less serious and funnier.

> **Brief note**
> A (movie) "director" is a person who makes movies.

B Vocabulary

Match the words in the box to the correct definitions.

a. vocational school / trade school	b. film school	c. medical school
d. junior college	e. law school	f. graduate school

1. _____ a school for future lawyers
2. _____ a school for future doctors
3. _____ a school for future moviemakers
4. _____ a two-year college that helps students prepare for university
5. _____ a school that teaches skills for a specific job (for example, mechanic)
6. _____ a school offering master's or PhD degrees

Expressions:

which... Use *which* to ask about one of many.
For example: ***Which*** *city do you live in?* There are many cities, but you live in only one.

the one... Use *the one* to be specific about which thing you're talking about.
For example, when asking for a book, someone says: *Give me* ***the one*** *on the left.*
In this sentence, *on the left* tells us which book the speaker is talking about.

C Grammar

> **Brief note**
> Choosing to use *a* or *an* depends on the first sound of the following word, not the first letter. So we say, for example, *I go to a university.*

Articles

no article	a/an	the
Don't use an article before an uncountable or plural noun when talking generally.	Use *a* or *an* for one countable noun when there isn't any context to know which one.	Any noun can use *the* if there is enough information or context.
Sugar is sweet. (This is true for all sugar, and sugar is uncountable.)	*Please give me* ***an*** *umbrella.* (I don't care which one. I want *any* umbrella.)	*Please give me* ***the*** *brown coat.* (*Brown* tells you which one I want. It is a specific one.)

places
• Most proper nouns do not take an article, but some do—especially places that sound like plurals or unions *(the Philippines, the United States, the United Kingdom)*, mountain ranges *(the Himalayas)*, seas, and oceans *(the Pacific Ocean)*. • Many places within a city or town take *the* even when they are not specific *(the library, the movie theater)*. We also use *the* with many natural areas *(the forest, the sea)*. • Some places—*church, school, home* (and *hospital* in British English)—do not take an article when we are talking about the function of the place. *(He is in school* means he is studying.)

D Grammar Practice

Fill in the blanks with *a*, *an*, or *the*. Put *x* if no article is needed. Discuss your answers with a partner.

1. I have _____ computer at my house in _____ United States of America, but not at my house in _____ France.

2. You have a lot of good books! Can I borrow _____ one about movie directors?

3. My cousin is going to _____ graduate school to be _____ architect.

4. Jim is having _____ spaghetti for _____ dinner tonight.

5. Is there _____ café near here? If so, do they have _____ good food?

6. How do you like _____ movie? I think it's awesome.

7. I'm going to _____ supermarket now.

8. Please close _____ door. _____ cold air is coming in.

9. Beth goes to _____ church every Sunday.

10. She wants to get _____ degree in physical education and become _____ teacher.

E Use the Language

Guessing game

List three things in each box below, but do not show your lists to anyone.

Countries	Cities	Sports	University Majors
1. _____	1. _____	1. _____	1. _____
2. _____	2. _____	2. _____	2. _____
3. _____	3. _____	3. _____	3. _____

When you are ready, find a partner and play a guessing game. (Do not show your list to your partner!)

- Your partner chooses a list—for example, the sports list.
- You give clues (pieces of information) about one of the things on that list. Your partner tries to guess what it is.
- Keep giving clues until your partner guesses right. Put a check mark next to that answer and switch roles.
- Which pair can checkmark every answer first?

A   Authentic Text: A college flyer

Read the flyer. Then listen. 🎧 Track 24

USC
UNIVERSITY OF SOUTHERN CALIFORNIA

Life on Campus

At the University of Southern California, there are over 40,000 students in undergraduate and graduate programs. Our students love their classes, but they also enjoy life outside the classroom. The campus is huge. There are several large, beautiful fountains. The oldest is right in front of the admissions building. Several dorms have large outdoor swimming pools. Students can relax outside on the quad or play games in the large Student Center. There are also gardens, theaters, and auditoriums. The campus is like a small city. How are sports at USC? Everybody loves the USC Trojans! They're one of the best American college football teams. The Trojans' stadium has seats for 93,000 fans!

Brief note

"Huge" means *very big*.

B   Vocabulary: Places on campus

Write the words from the box under the correct pictures.

garden	stadium	swimming pool	fountain
quad	dormitory (dorm)	theater	admissions building

1. _____

2. _____

3. _____

4. _____

5. _____

6. _____

7. _____

8. _____

C   In Your World

Talk to a partner about three different places that can be found on a college campus. What are those places like? What is there? Where are they on your campus? Describe them in detail and ask questions.

Grammar

there is and *there are; some* and *any*

there is	there are	some and any
Use *there is* for singular countable nouns and for uncountable nouns.	Use *there are* for plural countable nouns.	*Some* can be used with plural nouns or uncountable nouns, but *any* is usually used for negatives.
There is a tree in front of my house. **Is there** milk in the fridge?	**Are there** any cookies in the kitchen? **There are** many kinds of flowers.	There is **some** milk in the refrigerator. There aren't **any** apples in the kitchen.

Brief note

The subject *there* does not mean "in that place." It just means something exists.

E **Grammar Practice**

Put the words in order to make sentences.

1. no / water / in / the / pool / is / there / swimming

    _____.

2. engineering / in / there / women / your / any / class / are

    _____?

3. fountain / there / your / on / is / campus / a

    _____?

4. your / shirt / is / on / there / some / paint

    _____.

5. much / the / in / is / kitchen / there / food

    _____?

6. are / people / there / of / a lot / in / stadium / the

    _____.

F **Listen to Speak**

Listen to a short conversation about a campus. What is there at the woman's school? Put a check mark next to the correct places. ◉ **Track 25**

- [ ] a quad
- [ ] a stadium
- [ ] a theater
- [ ] a swimming pool
- [ ] dorms
- [ ] a student lounge

With a partner, write a conversation about your school. Practice it and then perform it for the class.

A   Model Conversation

Read the conversation. Then listen. 🔊 Track 26

Molly: I hear your university is very expensive.

Warren: Yeah, it is.

Molly: How much does it cost, if you don't mind my asking?

Warren: Tuition is over $50,000 a year. And there are a lot of other **expenses**—**housing**, books, a **meal plan**…

Molly: Wow. How do you **afford** it?

Warren: It's not easy, but I get some **scholarships**. I have some student **loans**, too.

Molly: Wow. I guess my school costs are reasonable, then.

Warren: How much do you pay?

Molly: The total for tuition and **fees** is $12,000 per year. And I live in a dorm room on campus. It's quite cheap.

B   Vocabulary

Write the bold words from the conversation next to the correct definitions.

1. _____ money that a person borrows that must be paid back
2. _____ a gift of money for education costs
3. _____ all the things a person has to spend money on
4. _____ a home, or the cost paid to live in a home
5. _____ the cost of a service
6. _____ money paid for a certain number of meals per month
7. _____ to have enough money for something

Expressions related to expense:

expensive:	costing a lot of money
not bad:	not costing very much money, but not cheap
reasonable:	not costing too much money; fair
cheap:	costing little money
It costs too much.	It's expensive. I can't afford it.
It doesn't cost much.	It's not expensive. It's cheap or reasonable. People can afford it.

> **Brief note**
> Sometimes, but not always, *cheap* means that something is low in quality.

C   In Your World

In your opinion, what is a reasonable price for each of the following? Write down your guess. Then compare with a partner.

a haircut: _____	a new car: _____	a seafood dinner: _____
one year of college: _____	a pair of jeans: _____	a diamond ring: _____

D Grammar

Proper nouns and capitalization

Proper nouns are the names of specific people, places, companies, streets, planets, etc.: *Alicia Rodriguez, Chicago, India, the United Kingdom, Friday, Microsoft.*

In English, do NOT capitalize:	DO capitalize:
• the names of the seasons: *spring, summer, fall/autumn, winter* • the names of school subjects or majors: *math, history, engineering, biology* • *sun, moon*	• the names of months and days of the week: *Monday, Friday, March, September* • the names of specific classes: *Asian History 101; Introduction to Art* • the names of planets: *Venus, Mars*

Brief note

The names of languages are always capitalized: *I'm taking French this semester.*

Titles of books, plays, songs, articles, works of art, etc., are proper nouns. They sometimes include an article, and they follow special capitalization rules:

- Always capitalize the first word in a title: *It's My Life; A Tale of Two Cities*
- Capitalize all the other nouns, pronouns, verbs, adjectives, and adverbs: *Cool It; Fast Car*
- Do NOT capitalize articles *(a, an, the)* or common prepositions *(of, to, at)* except for the first word: *The Life of Pi; Of Mice and Men; She's the One*

E Grammar Practice

Correct the sentences by capitalizing the correct words.

1. On thursday they're going to mexico city.

2. She goes to georgetown university. Her major is physical education.

3. Are you reading *the lord of the rings*?

4. We want to see the musical *the lion king*.

5. You can take computer engineering 305 in august.

6. I love this song! it's called *dancing in the street*.

F Use the Language

Which do you like?

Think about some English-language songs, movies, and TV shows that you like. List at least three of each. Then find a partner and check each other's work for correct capitalization.

Movies	Songs	TV Shows
1.	1.	1.
2.	2.	2.
3.	3.	3.

Talk about your lists. Which things do you and your partner agree about? Discuss the things you like.

A   Which school?

Listen to a conversation about three different schools. Use the details to fill in the blanks in the sentences below. 🔘Track 27

1. Nancy could go to the Monet Institute. It's a good school, but _____ is very _____. And there _____ _____ housing on campus.

2. She could _____ _____ the Fine Arts Academy of Memphis. _____ _____ a lot of great instructors there.

3. _____ last school is _____ small school in Vermont. It's called the New England Arts Institute. It's not expensive, there are _____ _____ students, and _____ _____ is beautiful.

Listen again. Make notes on some of the questions Nancy's friend asks her and Nancy's responses. 🔘Track 27

B   Comprehension

Answer the following questions.

1. What is Nancy trying to decide?
2. What doesn't she like about the Monet Institute?
3. What is the problem with the Fine Arts Academy of Memphis?
4. What is the problem with the New England Arts Institute?

C   Choosing a School

Discuss the conversation with a partner.

Which school do you think Nancy should go to? Why?
What other things should you think about when choosing a university?

D   Reminder

Some Module 2 Goals in Unit 3

Put a check mark (✓) next to the things you can do.

_____   Very simply describe where you go to school

_____   Describe your education

_____   Understand people if they speak very slowly and clearly about simple everyday topics

Read to Write

Read information about several university students, including the activities they often do and their comments about life on campus.

Name	Major	Activities	Comment
Michelle Brito	World Literature	• Read and discuss books with friends	"I like learning new things. I work hard to be the best in my class. I don't have much time for hobbies, but I have good conversations with other literature majors."
Tyrone Swinton	Elementary Education	• Practice baseball • Have fun with friends • Exercise	"I'm an education major, but I'm also a baseball player. I study a lot, but I practice a lot, too. I get a scholarship to play for the university team."
Denise Cobb	Fine Arts	• Practice dance • Dance for fun at the club • Study French and play piano	"I love what I do as a dance major. I also have other interests. I love practicing my French and my music."
Jaylynn Garcia	Business Administration	• Attend business classes • Work as a part-time cook	"I already have a part-time job at a restaurant. I'm learning about business to prepare for my future career. And I love to cook!"
Marcus Abbey	Engineering	• Study engineering and math • Fix my three old cars	"I want to be an engineer in a car company. On the weekends, I fix my old cars like a mechanic. I love to work with my hands."

B   **Speak to Write**

Talk to a partner about the daily lives of university students you know. Discuss students with some of the majors above and with some other majors that you know about.

C   **Now Write**

Choose one major. On a separate piece of paper, write everything you know about life for a student with that major. You have eight minutes.

When you finish, count the number of words in your writing. Report to your teacher. Then read it and correct any mistakes you find. How many mistakes are there? Report this to your teacher, too.

★ Unit 4 · College Life ★

Lesson 1 — Where is it?

A — Authentic Text: A letter to freshmen

Read the letter. Then listen. 🎧 Track 28

Welcome, freshmen!

We want to introduce you to the campus and help you learn where some things are.

One of the first things you see when you come into the front entrance is the large fountain in the middle of the south courtyard. Behind that is the admissions office. The science library is on the left, and on the right, next to the admissions office, is the administration building. The academic center, the housing office, and many other offices are inside.

There are two main paths out of the courtyard. The path between the science library and the admissions office takes you toward our athletic center and the food court. The wide path on the right, past the administration building, leads to the dormitories and the middle of campus. Around there are the academic buildings, where most classrooms are located.

Visit our information center to learn more about your new campus!

fountain

science library

administration building

> **Brief note**
> Something "academic" is related to school and studying.

B — Vocabulary: Around campus

Common Campus Locations			
laboratory (*or* lab)	student center	administration building	academic center
housing office	financial aid center	athletic center	food court
concert hall	garage	auditorium	courtyard

C — Vocabulary Comprehension

Look back at part B. Where can you find the following things? Discuss with a partner.

1. a place to exercise and play sports
2. music performances
3. help getting a place to live
4. an open area with buildings around it
5. information about clubs and social activities
6. parked cars
7. help with money to pay for college
8. offices of the president and college employees
9. places to eat
10. shows and speeches
11. science projects
12. tutors and counselors to give advice on classes

D — In Your World

Write one to three sentences about a place that you often go, such as your school. Where is it? What kind of transportation do you use to get there? Share your sentences with a partner.

_____

_____

Grammar

Prepositions of location

prepositions	examples
next to / beside	The library is **next to** the athletic center.
near	There is an information center **near** the dormitory.
in front of	Let's meet **in front of** the food court
behind	Do you know what's **behind** the auditorium?
around	There are a lot of buildings **around** the courtyard.
inside	The academic center is **inside** the administration building.
outside	A beautiful garden is **outside** my dormitory.
between ___ and ___	The fountain is **between** the admissions office **and** the courtyard.
on the right / left of	**On the left of** the housing office, you can find the president's office.
across ___ from / opposite	My office is **across** the hall **from** the financial aid center.

Brief note

We can say *across from...* or put a noun between those words in phrases like *across the street from...*

Grammar Practice

Circle the correct answers.

1. My nose is (next to / between) my eyes.

2. The dormitories are (between / around) the courtyard.

3. The auditorium is (opposite / across) the street from the post office.

4. Can you please move? I can't see what's (behind / around) you.

5. You live (on the right of / near) the bus stop, so you really don't need a car.

6. Why are these books (inside / outside) the library? They should be (inside / outside) on the shelves.

Put the words in order to make sentences.

7. sit / to / next / down / me / please   _____.

8. the / I / school / my / from / across / live / street   _____.

Use the Language

A campus and its surroundings

Ask your partner to describe the buildings and places on a college campus. Draw a simple map of the campus your partner describes. Then ask about some things that are around the outside of the campus and draw them.

Now show your map to your partner. Is it right?

Lesson 2 — I love doing experiments.

A — Model Conversation

Read the conversation. Then listen. 🎧 Track 29

Yolanda: What's your major?
Pete: I'm studying Russian language and literature.
Yolanda: Wow. How's that?
Pete: Well, reading Russian is a lot of fun. I understand it pretty well when I go slowly. But listening is really difficult for me.
Yolanda: Oh yeah? When I study foreign languages, reading is more difficult.
Pete: Not for me. Understanding a fast talker is hard. Anyway, what's your major?
Yolanda: I'm studying physics.
Pete: Oh, cool. What do you like about it?
Yolanda: I love doing experiments in the lab and research in the library. But I hate the lectures. They're boring. My professor talks too much.

> **Brief note**
> A "lecture" is an academic talk. In a lecture, the teacher speaks and the students listen.

B — Vocabulary: Activities and feelings

solving problems	doing experiments	taking notes	doing research

*I **like** solving math problems.* *like* = have a good feeling about	*I **love** doing science experiments.* *love* = a stronger feeling than *like*	*I **dislike** taking notes in class.* *dislike* = the opposite of *like*	*I **hate** doing research in the library.* *hate* = a stronger feeling than *dislike*

> **Brief note**
> It's more common to say *don't like* than *dislike*.

Fill in the blanks with the correct forms of the verbs. (Answers may vary.)

1. My chemistry class is great. I love _____ _____ in the laboratory.
2. I'm good at writing, but I _____ _____ notes in class. It's just not very fun for me.
3. Cassandra really _____ _____ mathematics problems. I asked her to help me with my math homework, and she got angry!
4. David is doing _____ for a history report. He doesn't _____ it, but he says it's not too bad.

C — In Your World

Talk to a partner about learning English. Talk about listening, speaking, reading, and writing.

Which is easy for you, and which is hard? Which is most important? Why?
What are some good ways to learn each of the language skills?

D Grammar

Gerunds

gerunds
A gerund looks like a verb with an *-ing* ending, but it is used like a noun. It can be a subject, or it can be the object of verbs such as *like* or *avoid*.

gerunds as subjects	gerunds as objects
Swimming is fun. **Reading** bores me. **Watching** horror movies scares me.	I like **swimming**. I don't enjoy **reading**. I avoid **watching** horror movies.

Brief note

The subject here is *watching*, and it is singular even though *horror movies* is plural.

some verbs with gerunds as objects				
like	dislike	avoid	consider	continue
love	enjoy	stop	start	practice
hate	prefer	quit	keep	imagine

E Grammar Practice

Put the words in order to make sentences.

1. homework / she / doing / avoids / her

   _____.

2. practicing / the / piano / continue / you / should

   _____.

3. spelling / English / is / hard / words

   _____.

4. they / cooking / hate / about / learning

   _____.

5. classmates / likes / David / working / his / with

   _____.

6. prefer / at / I / food court / eating / the

   _____.

F Use the Language

Likes and dislikes

Write a paragraph about things you like and don't like about school life. Include classroom activities, studying at home, social activities, clubs, and athletics. When you're finished, discuss your paragraph with a partner.

A   Model Conversation

Read the conversation. Then listen. Track 30

Nancy: Are you enjoying your semester?

Will: Yeah. I'm learning a lot and making friends. My roommate and I get along, too.

Nancy: Are you doing any extracurricular activities these days?

Will: Sure. I'm on a bowling team. We practice a lot on the weekends, so I'm improving my game. What about you?

Nancy: I'm in an English conversation club. We talk a lot about current events, news stories, movies—things like that.

Will: Are you doing it as part of a class?

Nancy: No. I'm taking English classes too, but the club is just for fun. We don't study—it's just chatting. My listening and speaking skills are really improving.

Will: That sounds great. Can I join?

B   Vocabulary

Write the words and phrases next to the correct definitions.

improve	roommate	currently	club	skill	join
extracurricular activity	current event	at the moment	get along	chat	these days

1. something you choose to do at school but not for a class _____
2. the ability to do something   _____
3. something happening recently or not long ago   _____
4. a social group for people with the same interest   _____
5. a person you live with   _____
6. to get better or make (something) better   _____
7. to become a member of (a club, team, etc.)   _____
8. to like each other; to enjoy being with each other   _____
9. to make conversation   _____
10. three phrases meaning *at this time* _____   _____   _____

C   In Your World

Answer the questions in one or two sentences.

1. Are you currently learning anything new? _____

   _____

2. Who do you not get along with? _____

   _____

Grammar

Present continuous and related time expressions

statements: S + *be* + verb-*ing*...	
They **are talking** to their professor right now.	I'm not **studying** mathematics this semester.
yes/no questions: *Be* + S + verb-*ing*...?	
Are you **going** to class this morning?	**Is** she **doing** any extracurricular activities?
when and how to use present continuous	
• Use the present continuous to talk about what is happening right now. • Use it to talk about something that is current and temporary. For example: *I'm learning to play the violin—not at this moment, but these days. I'm living in the dormitory this semester.* Both of these sentences bring attention to something current. • Present continuous sentences often use expressions about a recent or current time.	
common time expressions	
now, at the moment, right now, today, tonight, nowadays, this ____ (minute, morning, week, semester, year)	

E **Grammar Practice**

Fill in the blanks to make questions. Match the questions and answers. Then fill in the blanks to complete the answers.

1. _____ he reading a book? •
2. _____ they studying Arabic this semester? •
3. _____ my singing improving? •
4. _____ I asking too many questions? •

• **a.** No, _____ not.
• **b.** Yes, _____ getting much better!
• **c.** Yes, _____ _____ a history book.
• **d.** No, _____ not _____ any language.

Now look back at the conversation in part A and circle all the words that end in -*ing*. Which are gerunds, and which are verbs? List three examples of each in the box below.

gerunds (used as nouns)	-*ing* verbs (used with *be*)

F **Use the Language**

These days

• Write a short list of things you're doing these days. What are you studying? How are you spending your free time? Keep your list a secret—don't show it to anyone!

• Find a partner. Give hints to help your partner guess some things on your list.

• Try to guess what your partner is doing these days. Then ask for some details.

I kick a ball with my friends at the athletic center.

So are you practicing soccer these days?

That's right, I am.

Do you play often?

A Model Conversation

Read the conversation. Then listen. ⊙ Track 31

Stacy: Why are you taking an economics class this semester? Aren't you a history major?

Brad: I am. Studying economics helps me understand a lot of historical events. Money is important, you know.

Stacy: Haha. I do know. What other classes are you taking?

Brad: For my major, I'm taking a class called South America in the 1800s.

Stacy: Huh. That sounds like a good elective for me. Who's the teacher?

Brad: Professor Williams. This week we're doing group presentations about industry and agriculture.

Stacy: How are you doing in that class?

Brad: I'm doing all right. I like the topic, but Professor Williams gives us a lot of extra reading assignments. Sometimes it's hard to keep up.

B Vocabulary

Write the words next to the correct definitions.

keep up	topic	industry	agriculture
historical	presentation	elective	assignment

1. work that a teacher or boss tells you to do   _____

2. the making or building of things in a factory   _____

3. related to history   _____

4. what a class, lecture, book, etc. is about; a subject   _____

5. a course not related to your major that you can choose to study   _____

6. to move or work at the same speed as others; to go fast enough   _____

7. farming; the raising of crops   _____

8. a short talk about a topic, sometimes by a student or group of students _____

C In Your World

Think about one of your academic goals—for example, to learn another language or to improve your grades in a subject. Fill in the table below. Then discuss your goal with a partner.

My Goal: _____	
Good things about this goal:	Difficult things about this goal:
_____	_____
_____	_____
_____	_____

Grammar

Present continuous in information questions

information questions: *Wh-* word + *be* + S + verb-*ing*...?		
questions	short answers	long answers
Where are we **going**? **What** classes **is** she **taking**? **How are** you **doing** in that class? **Why are** you **leaving**?	To the food court. History and economics. All right. Because I have class now.	We're going **to the food court**. She's taking **history and economics**. I'm doing **all right**. I'm leaving **because I have class now**.
subject questions: *Who* + *be* + verb-*ing*...?		
Who's teaching that class?	Professor Williams (is).	**Professor Williams** is teaching it.

Brief note

Present continuous questions can often be answered with just the subject, the matching form of *be*, and, if necessary, the word *not*.

E **Grammar Practice**

Write the beginning of each question below, including the correct form of *be*. One question is a yes/no question. Others use a word from the box below.

who	what	when	where	how	why

1. Q: _____ _____ you taking that class? A: Every weekday morning.
2. Q: _____ _____ he improving his English? A: He's taking a conversation class.
3. Q: _____ they sleeping? A: Yes, they are.
4. Q: _____ _____ you reading? A: I'm reading a science book.
5. Q: _____ _____ you carrying a guitar? A: Because I'm in a music club.
6. Q: _____ _____ Tom and Sarah going? A: To the financial aid center.
7. Q: _____ _____ talking on the phone? A: My roommate is.

F **Read to Speak**

Prepare to discuss some current events with your classmates. Research a few news stories about things that are happening in the world, and think of events at your school or in your city, too. Copy the headlines of some news stories about these events below.

_____

_____

_____

_____

G **Use the Language**

What's going on?

Now talk with other students in groups of two to five. Talk about what is happening in your school, your community, and your country. Ask and answer follow-up questions to get more details. You can follow this with a further discussion of what is going on internationally.

A Authentic Text: A club poster

Read the poster. Then listen. 🔵 Track 32

THE WYOMING STATE UNIVERSITY HORSE RIDING CLUB is looking for new members—and we want **YOU**!

We love horses. Do you? Then join us! We always have something exciting happening—every day of the week. Senior members of our club teach horse care, riding, and sports involving horses. We often have group rides, and you can always find a riding partner. This semester, our university is building a larger riding area, and it is opening in April. Do you want to take part in something really special? We usually have two riding events per semester, and more than twenty horses and riders participate. We hope to see you and your beautiful horse at a Horse Riding Club meeting soon!

Brief note

"Take part in" and *participate in* have the same meaning.

For more information, call 555-722-6262 or email at joinclub@wyomingacademic.com.

B Vocabulary

Fill in the blanks with the correct words from the box. Circle the correct adverbs of frequency.

special	take part	involving	event	participate	per

Adverbs of Frequency						
never	hardly ever	occasionally	sometimes	often	usually	always

1. Today is a(n) _____ day—we're watching a movie in class. We (often / hardly ever) watch movies!
2. I don't have time to _____ in club activities. I (occasionally / always) study after classes and on weekends.
3. There's a social _____ at the dorm every Friday night. It's (usually / never) a lot of fun!
4. Samantha loves doing experiments _____ chemistry. She's (hardly ever / often) at the laboratory.
5. The classes at my college are (never / sometimes) very big. There are only about twenty students _____ class, and the biggest classes have around thirty.

C In Your World

Talk with a partner about the extracurricular activities below. What do you think the members do? Which one would you like to join, and which would you not like to join? Explain your choices.

Skiing Team	School Newspaper	Hip-Hop Club
Yoga Club	Creative Writing Club	Future Business Leaders

D Quick Review

Look back at the brief notes in this module.

1. Which word has a different meaning than the others?   job   occupation   lecture   career
2. To ask about someone's (occupation / department), say (What do you do? / What are you doing?)

Grammar

Brief note

A *routine* is the things you usually do and the order you do them in.

Simple present vs. present continuous

simple present	present continuous

Use for routines:
  *I **take** the bus to school every day.*
Use for facts that are generally true at all times:
  *Students **study**.*
	Use for something happening now:
	  *Harry **is talking** with his sociology professor.*
	Use for something current and temporary:
	  *I'**m learning** a lot this semester.*

stative verbs	

- Many verbs do not describe an action. Examples include *be* and *hate*. These verbs are called stative verbs. We usually use stative verbs in the simple present tense, NOT in the present continuous.
- Stative verbs include most verbs that discuss what you know, think, or feel (*I **like** this soup.*), what you believe (*I don't **believe** you.*), what you see or hear (*I **see** a snake!*), what you own (*I **have** a car.*), or just ways of being. They don't discuss actions.

Brief note

A good way to learn which verbs do not use present continuous is by listening to how native English speakers use them.

Brief note

Some stative verbs can be used in the present continuous tense when they imply an action.
I'm having lunch with my friend.
I'm thinking of my mom now.

F **Grammar Practice**

Fill in the blanks with the correct forms of the verbs.

1. (like)   Carlos _____ playing soccer.
2. (watch)   At the moment, I _____ a video lecture.
3. (study)   They _____ for next week's test.
4. (sit)   That's her. She _____ near the back of the class.
5. (know)   _____ you _____ a lot about geography?
6. (fit)   This jacket _____ not _____ me well.
7. (believe) We _____ exercising every day is good for you.
8. (have)   He _____ many cousins.
9. (rain)   Look out the window. _____ it _____?
10. (work)   I _____, so I can't meet you for lunch today.

G **Use the Language**

How often?

Ask a partner these questions and mark his or her responses in the table. Follow up by asking a few questions of your own.

Questionnaire: How often do you do the following? (Put a check mark in the correct box.)	Always	Often	Sometimes	Never
1. go home right after school	☐	☐	☐	☐
2. copy class notes from a classmate	☐	☐	☐	☐
3. study outside with classmates	☐	☐	☐	☐
4. eat lunch in a school cafeteria	☐	☐	☐	☐
5. participate in class discussions	☐	☐	☐	☐
6. attend a club/team meeting	☐	☐	☐	☐

When both you and your partner have completed your questionnaires, survey your other classmates and compare the results. Survey the entire class. What answers did most students give? Is there anything that everyone always does? Is there something that nobody ever does?

A An Educational Questionnaire

Read the completed questionnaire. Then put a check mark next to true or false.

1. What is your name? _____Gary Jackson_____

2. Are you currently a student? (Y/N) __No__

    If yes, then what is your current grade or year in university? _____ Class of _____

    What are you studying? _____

    Which school are you attending? _____

    If no, then what is the name of the last school you attended? _New York University_

    Did you graduate? _Yes_   Class of _2012_

    What was your major? _____Film Studies_____

3. What is the highest level of education you completed?
    _____Graduated university with a bachelor's degree_____

1.	Gary is currently attending university.	☐ true	☐ false
2.	Gary finished graduate school in 2012.	☐ true	☐ false
3.	Gary studied movies.	☐ true	☐ false

Write more questions about what someone is currently doing at school, studying, etc., to add to the survey. Leave the answers blank for now.

4. _____ ?

    _____ .

5. _____ ?

    _____ .

6. _____ ?

    _____ .

B An Oral Survey

Interview a partner to get his or her answers to your survey questions above. Ask and answer using complete sentences. Then write short, simple answers based on your partner's responses.

C Reminder

Some Module 2 Goals in Unit 4

Put a check mark (✓) next to the things you can do.

_____ Find basic information in posters or advertisements

_____ Describe what you like doing and don't like (for example, with regard to school)

_____ Complete a questionnaire with information about your educational background

A Listen to Write

For a class assignment, Wendy is writing a paragraph about what she is doing these days. Read, listen, and fill in the blanks. 🔘 Track 33

I _____ high school last spring, and now I'm a freshman at Penn State. I _____ _____ in world history. _____ _____ in a dormitory _____ the Weaver Building. Many of my history classes are in that building. I _____ walk along the path between the library and the theater to get to class. But _____ _____ _____ off campus to visit a café before classes. _____, I don't have much time to spend in the café. That's because _____ _____ for a big midterm test this week, so I'm spending a lot of time in the library between classes. And I _____ stay in my dorm room in the evenings to study. Last semester, I was in the Spanish _____ and on the basketball team. But now I'm very busy, so I'm not _____ in extracurricular activities much _____ _____. I _____ need a break from studying, so I meet my friends to have coffee or lunch and to _____.

B Prewrite

Use the space below to list five or six of your recent activities. Then select the three most interesting ones and think about how to describe them.

C Now Write

Write a short paragraph about your recent activities. Look back at part A for help if necessary.

Module 2 Review

A Vocabulary

Choose the correct answers.

1. A second-year university student is a(n) _____.
   a. sophomore   b. senior   c. academic   d. professor

2. A _____ is a place where most of a college's buildings are located.
   a. campus   b. courtyard   c. quad   d. scholarship

3. Borrowed money is a(n) _____.
   a. program   b. tuition   c. expense   d. loan

4. _____ is the study of beauty, makeup, and hair styling.
   a. Cosmetology   b. Yoga   c. Physics   d. Psychology

5. Class schedules can be found in the _____.
   a. courtyard   b. dormitories   c. admissions office d. financial aid center

6. A class you can choose to take, but don't have to take, is a(n) _____.
   a. major   b. minor   c. elective   d. lecture

7. A club or social activity that you do outside of classes is a(n) _____ activity.
   a. expense   b. expensive   c. elective   d. extracurricular

8. _____ is the study of farming and crops.
   a. Academic   b. Agriculture   c. Admissions   d. Administration

B Grammar

Underline the errors and write the correct word(s) on the lines.

1. A money is important. I really need some money these days. _____

2. He avoids ride his bike around campus. _____

3. How much classes are you taking this semester? _____

4. You doing any extracurricular activities this month? _____

5. Kevin is knowing a lot about philosophy. _____

6. Watch movies with friends is fun. _____

7. What do you work? _____

8. I asked him several question. He answered all of them. _____

9. My dormitory is across the street the campus bookstore. _____

10. I want to study English in United States or UK. _____

11. My friend goes to the university of southern California. _____

C Which major?

With a partner, take turns role-playing the part of an academic counselor.

1. Ask your partner what he or she likes and dislikes doing.
2. What does he or she enjoy learning about?
3. Suggest three different majors for your partner to think about.
4. Help your partner choose which of the three would be best to study.

D Beyond the Classroom

Talk in a group of two to five students. Discuss things that university students often do outside the classroom.

Where do they go? What do they do there?

What off-campus places and activities are popular?

Why do students do these things?

What do you think of these out-of-class activities?

E Perfect University

Working with partners, talk about ideas for a perfect university. What majors should it offer? What clubs and extracurricular activities? Discuss the buildings and other places on campus.

Based on your discussion, write a list of this perfect university's features. Then write a detailed description of the campus, including the locations of important buildings and other things on campus.

Name your university, and present your ideas to the class.

University Name: _____

Majors	Describe the campus
Activities	
Places	

From School to Home

Module 3 Goals

Ask and answer questions about where people live

Build on a basic vocabulary of words and phrases to talk about yourself and
communicate in common everyday situations

Understand simple directions for getting from X to Y on foot or by public transport

Ask people how they feel in different situations and say how you feel

Write simple sentences about yourself (for example, where you live)

Indicate time by such phrases as *last Friday*

Find the most important information in timetables, etc.

Describe your home and where you live

Module ❸ Preview

Preview

Look at pages 64 to 89. What pages are these things on?

a crossword puzzle   _____

a movie schedule   _____

advertisements for apartments   _____

a man talking on a cell phone   _____

Write and Discuss

Write your answers to the questions. Then talk about them with a partner.

1. Where do you live?

2. How do you get around town?

3. What do you like best about your neighborhood?
    I really like the …

4. What do you like least?

5. What type of place do you want to live in?
    I want to live in a place with …

Unit 5

Unit 6

Scan the QR code to watch a preview video.

63

Lesson 1 — From Home to School

A Model Conversation

Read the conversation. Then listen. 🔊 Track 34

Sarah: Hey, Enzo. You're late again. In fact, you're later than yesterday.

Enzo: I know. I come to school by train, and it takes a long time.

Sarah: I come on the subway. It's faster than the train.

Enzo: Yeah, but there's no subway stop near my place.

Sarah: Too bad. You need to find an apartment closer to school.

Enzo: I think you're right. I need to find one that's less expensive, too.

Sarah: I think there are some empty apartments in my building. It's cheaper than your place. I can ask the landlord.

Enzo: Thanks. That sounds great.

> **Brief note**
> A "landlord" is a person who owns a place that other people rent.

B Vocabulary

Listen to the conversation again. Circle the types of transportation you hear. 🔊 Track 34

(by) plane

(by) train

(by) car

(by) bicycle/bike

(by) subway

on foot (walk)

(by) boat

(by) taxi

Fill in the blanks with the correct type of transportation.

1. This travels on the water: _____
2. This goes underground: _____
3. This has two wheels: _____
4. This flies: _____
5. This is a kind of car: _____

C In Your World

Choose a partner. Ask and answer the question below. Then write your partner's answer.

What is your favorite way to travel? Why?

_____

_____

D Grammar

Comparison with adjectives

Brief note

To form the comparative of a one-syllable adjective ending in a silent *e*, add -*r*: *nice – nicer*. To form the comparative of an adjective ending in consonant-vowel-consonant, double the final consonant: *big – bigger*.

comparison to a higher degree (comparative forms)			
one syllable adjective + -*er*	**adjectives ending in -*y*** -*y* to -*ier*	**two or more syllables** *more* + adjective	**irregular**
high – high**er** small – small**er**	pretty – prett**ier** happy – happ**ier**	**more** interesting **more** expensive	good – **better** bad – **worse**

comparison to a lower degree			
option 1: *less* + adjective		option 2: *not as* _____ *as*	
less interesting **less** healthy **less** smart **less** capable		**not as** big **as** **not as** expensive **as** **not as** pretty **as** **not as** rich **as**	

Brief note

When the people or things are the same, say *as* + adj. + *as*: *I'm as tall as him.*

Brief note

To compare two people or things, you usually need *than*: *She's taller than him. He's less healthy than she is.* But don't use *than* with *not as*: *He's not as tall as her.*

E Grammar Practice

Fill in the blanks with the correct form of the adjective, in the degree indicated.

1. silly (higher) _____
2. boring (higher) _____
3. hard (higher) _____
4. large (lower) _____
5. difficult (lower) _____
6. easy (higher) _____

Of the phrases you wrote, which two have the same meaning? _____

Read the sentences. Fill in the blanks with the comparative forms of the adjectives. Use each word only once, and use the Internet if necessary.

long	tall	expensive	fast	small

7. The Nile River is _____ than the Amazon.
8. Ferraris are _____ than Hyundais.
9. A mouse is _____ than a dog.
10. Mount Everest is _____ than Mount Kilimanjaro.
11. A horse is _____ than a person.

F Use the Language

Talk about traveling

How do you travel? Write your answers in the chart. Then ask a partner and write your partner's answers.

How do you...	You	Your partner
...get to school?		
...get home?		
...go somewhere on vacation?		
...go downtown?		

A   Model Conversation

Read the conversation. Then listen. 🔊 Track 35

Michelle: That was an interesting lecture.

Aiden: Yeah, but confusing. I'm going to go ask the professor a few questions.

Michelle: You should do that. She's amazing. She's always ready to help.

Aiden: That's good to know. Are you heading home?

Michelle: Yeah, finally. Wednesday is always tiring for me—five classes, and the first one is at 8:30.

Aiden: Wow, that's a long day.

Michelle: And now I have to ride the bus for an hour. But it's relaxing. I just listen to music. Tomorrow is shorter, too, and my classes start late. I can sleep a lot and still get to class on time.

> **Brief note**
> "On time" means *not late*.

B   Vocabulary

Listen to the conversation again. Circle the words that Aiden says. Put a check mark by the words that Michelle says. 🔊 Track 35

boring

interesting

exciting

relaxing

confusing

annoying

tiring

amazing

C   About You

Choose the word that best describes each activity.

1. **studying English:**   boring   tiring   exciting   confusing   interesting
2. **playing soccer:**   exciting   relaxing   tiring   boring   amazing
3. **going skiing:**   relaxing   interesting   amazing   tiring   exciting
4. **going shopping:**   boring   amazing   interesting   exciting   tiring

Find a partner. Compare your answers. Do you agree or disagree?

Now discuss these questions with your partner.

How do you feel right now?   What activities are relaxing for you?

What is annoying about school?

Grammar

Review of *-ing* forms and introduction to *-ing* adjectives

uses of *-ing* forms		
They can be used as **nouns**. For example: ***Walking** is good for your health*. When an *-ing* form is used as a noun, it is called a **gerund**.	They can be used as main **verbs**. For example: *I am **studying** English*.	Some of them can be used as **adjectives** to describe a person, thing, or situation that causes a feeling. For example: *Science is **interesting***. Not all *-ing* forms can be used as adjectives.
More on *-ing* adjectives		
Like most adjectives, *-ing* adjectives can be used before nouns or after linking verbs.		
Play some **relaxing** music.		That new student seems **interesting**.

Brief note

See p. 73 for more on linking verbs.

Grammar Practice

Look at the underlined word. Write *G* for gerund, *V* for verb, or *A* for adjective.

1. _____ <u>Eating</u> healthy food is important.

2. _____ I am <u>watching</u> a good series on TV.

3. _____ Is the subway <u>arriving</u> at the platform?

4. _____ The family that moved in next door is very <u>annoying</u>.

5. _____ Tommy really likes <u>running</u>, but not in marathons.

6. _____ I love this course because the professor is always <u>interesting</u>.

Use the Language

What's happening?

Look at the pictures. What do you think is happening? Why does the person feel this way? Write a sentence about each picture.

_____

_____

_____

_____

Choose one picture. Then find a partner. Do not tell your partner which picture you are talking about, but describe what you think is happening in the picture. Your partner will try to guess which picture you are describing.

A   Model Conversation

Read the conversation. Then listen. 🎧 Track 36

Landlord: Hello?

Steve: Hello, I'm calling about the apartment in the advertisement online. Is it still available?

Landlord: Yes, it is.

Steve: Great. How far is it from Richfield College?

Landlord: It's ten kilometers or so. Go straight on College Road until you reach North Street. Turn left on North and keep going for seven blocks until you reach Capital Road. The apartment is on the corner of Capital and North.

Steve: Oh. It's quite far from the college. How close is it to the subway?

Landlord: There's a subway stop three blocks away.

Steve: Okay. Thank you for the information.

> **Brief note**
> "Or so" means around, but not exactly.

B   Vocabulary

Listen to the conversation again. Four of the phrases below appear in the conversation. Number the pictures 1, 2, 3, and 4 in the order that you hear the phrases. 🎧 Track 36

turn left

go straight

turn right

on the corner

one block

across the street from

beside / next to

between

C   About You

Write three sentences describing the location of your home. Use the expressions in the box or your own ideas. Share your sentences with a partner.

one block from / two blocks from	across the street from	beside / next to	between

My apartment / house / dorm is _____

_____

_____

Grammar

How + adjective questions and answers

How	adjective...?	Answer directly or with a comparative, a superlative, or an intensifier.
How	**expensive** is the rent? **close** is it to the subway? **big** is the apartment? **far** is it from the school?	It's about $400 a month. (directly) It's closer than my old apartment. (comparative) It's the biggest one in the neighborhood. (superlative) It's quite close—one hundred meters or so away. (intensifier)

E **Grammar Practice**

Read the sentence. Write a question using How to find out more information.

1. There are two bedrooms. (big)

   _____.

2. This hotel seems nice. (close to downtown)

   _____.

3. I'm reading a book in English. (difficult)

   _____.

4. I want to buy these shoes. (expensive)

   _____.

F **Use the Language**

Where do you live?

Draw a map from your classroom to where you live or work. Then find a partner. Ask your partner to close his or her book and explain how he or she gets from class to home or work. Draw a map of what your partner says.

My map:	My partner's map:

When you finish drawing your partner's map, close your book. Describe to your partner how you get from class to home or work as your partner draws a map of what you say in his or her book.

When your partner finishes drawing, open your books. Do your maps and your partner's maps look similar?

A Authentic Text: A newspaper advertisement

Read the advertisement. Then listen to the monologue. 🎧 Track 37

North End (college area)

For rent: 3 bdrm apt. Furnished. Util incl. $1200/mth. No pets. Call 562-1313 after 6 p.m. Avail immed.

For rent: Studio apt. Small pets welcome $500/mth. Email rentime@apt.com. Avail June 1st.

For rent: Small 1 bdrm apt. Next to subway. Shopping nearby. $600/mth. Internet, util incl. No pets.

Christopher: I have three apartments on my list, but one of them is clearly the best of the three. It's smaller than my apartment now—in fact, it's the smallest apartment on the list. But it's closest to school. It's next to the back gate, so it's in an exciting area. The apartment I like isn't the cheapest, but heat and lights are included in the rent, and I don't have to pay extra for the Internet. It's close to the subway and is nearest to the station where I work, so getting to work will be no problem.

B Vocabulary

Listen to the conversation again. What words do you hear? 🎧 Track 37

heat

lights

furnished

unfurnished

> **Brief note**
>
> The prefix *un-* means *not*. So *unfurnished* means *not furnished*.

C Vocabulary: Apartment ads

Match the words to the correct abbreviations.

a. included	b. available	c. month	d. bedroom	e. utilities	f. apartment	g. immediately
___ bdrm	___ util	___ incl	___ apt	___ avail	___ immed	___ mth

D Pronunciation

Word stress

Listen to the words. Circle the stressed syllable. 🎧 Track 38

1. in-clu-ded   **2.** a-vai-la-ble   **3.** u-ti-li-ties   **4.** a-part-ment   **5.** im-me-di-ate-ly

Listen again and repeat each word with the correct stress. 🎧 Track 38

E Grammar

Superlative adjectives

Brief note

Generally, we use *the* before a superlative. Sometimes, especially when there's no noun after the superlative, we don't.

superlatives for the highest degree			
one syllable adjective + *-est*	**adjectives ending in *-y*** *-y* to *-iest*	**two or more syllables** most + adjective	**irregular**
big – big**est** small – small**est**	pretty – prett**iest** happy – happ**iest**	**most** interesting **most** expensive	good – **best** bad – **worst**
superlatives for the lowest degree			
least + adjective	**least** interesting, **least** healthy, **least** capable, **least** smart		

F Grammar Practice

Read the chart. Complete the sentences using the correct forms of the adjectives.

Apartments: pros (✔) and cons (✗)							
	Apartment 1		Apartment 2		Apartment 3	
Rent	$500 per month	✔	$1200 per month	✗	$600 per month	✔
Location	20 km from school	✗	next to school	✔	5 km from school	✔
Size	studio—no bedroom	✗	3 bedrooms	✗	1 bedroom	✔
Transportation to school	by train	✗	on foot	✔	by subway	✔
Neighborhood	no shops nearby	✗	some expensive shops	✗	shops, restaurants, and entertainment	✔
My choice	✗		✗		✔	

1. Apartment 1 is the _____ (expensive).
2. Apartment 2 is the _____ (close) to school.
3. Apartment 2 is the _____ (large) apartment.
4. Apartment 3 is _____ (big) than Apartment 1.
5. Apartment 3 is _____ (cheap) than Apartment 2.

G Use the Language

Ranking

It can be hard to choose a new house or apartment. There are many different factors (things to consider). Look at the list of factors on the right. Try to add at least one more item to the list. Put the factors in order from most important to least important. Then compare your list with a partner's.

_____ price

_____ size

_____ near subway or bus

_____ neighborhood

_____ near shops and restaurants

_____ patio or green space

_____ safety

_____ _____

_____ _____

A Model Conversation

Read the conversation. Then listen. 🎧 Track 39

Emily: Hi, Nicholas. I hear you have a new apartment. I'm happy for you.

Nicholas: Thanks, Emily. I'm happy, too, but I'm also feeling a bit stressed. Moving is lots of work.

Emily: Yeah, you look stressed. When are you moving?

Nicholas: Next weekend.

Emily: Oh, no—right before exams. How do you feel about that?

Nicholas: I'm nervous about it. But I don't have a choice.

Emily: Yeah, it seems you don't. Well, do you need any help moving? Let me know.

> **Brief note**
> "Lots of" is an informal way of saying *a lot of*.

B Vocabulary: Feelings

Listen to the conversation again. Write an *E* by the words Emily says. Write an *N* by the words Nicholas says. 🎧 Track 39

1. When things are going well, you feel **happy**. _____
2. When you are alone and you hear a strange noise, you feel **afraid**. _____
3. When your sister loses your phone, you feel **angry**. _____
4. When you don't get enough sleep, you feel **tired**. _____
5. When someone you love dies, you feel **sad**. _____
6. When something unexpected happens, you feel **surprised**. _____
7. When you get a bad grade on a test, you feel **upset**. _____
8. Before a test, you feel **nervous**. _____

C In Your World

Complete the sentences. Then compare your answers with a partner.

	You	Your partner
I feel nervous when…		
I feel happy when…		
I'm angry when…		
I'm afraid when…		
I'm upset when…		
I feel sad when…		
I get tired when…		
I'm surprised when…		

Grammar

Linking verbs

linking verbs
Linking verbs connect a subject with information about that subject. They are not action verbs. An adjective can follow a linking verb, and a noun can follow some linking verbs (*be, become, remain*). Some verbs are always linking verbs. Others can be both action verbs and linking verbs.
"true" linking verbs (verbs that can only be linking verbs)
be, become, seem: *He **is** tired.*   *She **seems** angry.*   *We **are becoming** friends.*
common verbs that can be action verbs or linking verbs
look, remain, smell, sound, taste, turn, stay, get, appear, feel, grow: *The students **look** bored.*   *This room **smells** bad.*   *Her forehead **feels** hot.*
Is it an action verb or a linking verb?

Look at what follows the verb. Is it an object or an adjective?
     Action verb: *The chef **tastes** the soup.* (The noun *soup* is the object of the verb *tastes*.)
     Linking verb: *The soup **tastes** bad.* (*Bad* is an adjective.)

Grammar Practice

Read the sentences. Underline the linking verbs and circle the action verbs.

1. Giovanni reads the newspaper every morning. When he does, he feels sad.

2. My sister gets angry when people are rude to me.

3. The children on the playground are noisy as they play.

4. Caroline looks tired this morning. She goes to bed late these days.

5. The prices here seem very high. Let's go to another store.

6. My father gets a new book from the library every week. He likes to read.

7. I smelled the flowers. They smelled good.

Use the Language

What's the story?

Work with a partner. Look at the pictures.

With your partner, choose two or three of the pictures. Write a story to connect the people in them. Ask yourselves: How do the people feel? Why do they feel that way? What is happening?

Write a story, and then share it with your class.

A   Calling a Landlord

Listen to Christopher ask questions about apartments. Fill in the blanks with the missing information. Track 40

Conversation 1	Conversation 2
Christopher: Hello. I'm calling about the apartment in today's paper. Is it still available?	**Christopher:** Hello. I'm calling about the apartment for rent. Is it still available?
Landlord: Yes, it is. The rent is _____ a month.	**Landlord:** Yes, it is. It's _____ a month.
Christopher: Where's it located?	**Christopher:** What's the address?
Landlord: _____ South Road. The apartment is number _____.	**Landlord:** It's _____ East Avenue, apartment _____.
Christopher: Could I come by tomorrow at _____ to have a look?	**Christopher:** Can I come to see it tomorrow at _____?
Landlord: Yes. Call me when you get near. The number is _____.	**Landlord:** Yes. Text me when you get here. The number is _____.

Find and underline two answers for each question.

What does Christopher say to start the conversation with the landlord?

How does he ask about the location?

How does he make an appointment to see the apartment?

Brief note

Notice the different ways of including an apartment number in an address.

B   Discussing Apartments

Work with a partner. One person is calling about apartments, and the other person is the landlord. Use the information from the chart to have a conversation.

Price	Address	Time	Phone number
$600	4332 Queen Street #7	3 p.m.	413-665-2158
$450	18996 45th Avenue, apt. 9	9:30 a.m.	516-433-9234
$675	#14, 4591 Park Lane	7 p.m.	902-544-7610

C   Reminder

Some Module 3 Goals in Unit 5

Put a check mark (✓) next to the things you can do.

_____ Ask and answer questions about where people live

_____ Understand simple directions for getting from X to Y on foot or by public transport

_____ Build on a basic vocabulary of words and phrases to talk about yourself and communicate in common everyday situations

Read the Map Toolkit and Legend. Are there any words you don't know? Discuss what they mean with your teacher or look them up in a dictionary.

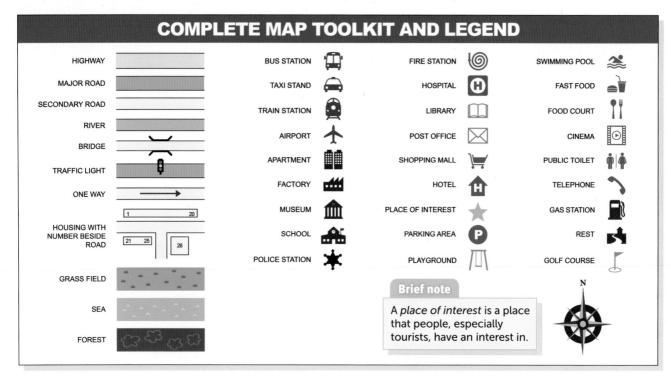

Choose five items from the Map Toolkit and Legend. Draw the items on the town map below.

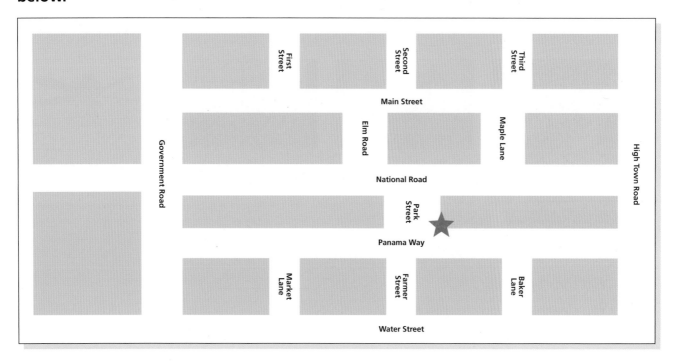

Find a partner. Do not let your partner see your map, and don't look at your partner's map. Your partner starts at the red star. Give him or her directions to the location of your items. When you are finished, check whether your partner found the correct location.

★ Unit 6 · At Home ★

Lesson 1 — A New Apartment

A Model Conversation

Read the conversation. Then listen. 🔘 Track 41

David: Hi, Paolo. How was your weekend?

Paolo: Hey, David. Not bad, but I was really busy. I moved into a new apartment.

David: Oh, yeah? Why?

Paolo: My old one was too far from school. The new one is next to a subway station, and it's closer to stores and restaurants, too.

David: How big is it?

Paolo: Well, it's smaller than my old apartment. The old one was really big. Anyway, there's a nice kitchen in the new one. It has a great view of the city, and there's a home office, too.

David: That sounds great.

Paolo: It is. Here's a picture of the view. Hey, meet me after class and I can take you there.

David: Sure. See you after class, then.

B Vocabulary

Listen to the conversation again. Circle the words you hear. 🔘 Track 41

balcony	sink	bathtub	rug

burner

stove	home office	view	ceiling fan

C Vocabulary Comprehension

Read the description and write the correct word from part B.

1. You cook on this. _____

2. You clean your body in this. _____

3. This keeps a room cool. _____ _____

4. You work here. _____ _____

5. You wash your hands here. _____

6. This is on the floor. _____

7. You can sit outside here and relax. _____

8. You see this from your window. _____

D Grammar

Simple past of *be*

Brief note

In the past tense, the *be* verb for first and third person singular subjects (*I, he, she, it*) is *was*. For all other subjects, use *were*.

simple present: *is/are*		simple past: *was/were*	
questions	answers	questions	answers
Is your new apartment big?	Yes, it **is**. No, it **isn't**.	**Was** your old apartment big?	Yes, it **was**. No, it **wasn't**.
Are the neighbors friendly?	Yes, they **are**. No, they **aren't**.	**Were** you guys busy over the weekend?	Yeah, we **were**. No, we **weren't**.

E Grammar Practice

Circle the correct form of *be* to complete the questions and answers.

1. Q: (Is / Was) the old apartment nice?   A: Yes, it (is / was).
2. Q: (Are / Were) your old neighbors friendly?   A: No, they (aren't / weren't).
3. Q: (Is / Was) the kitchen in the old apartment small?   A: Yes, it (is / was).
4. Q: (Is / Was) the old apartment more expensive?   A: No, it (isn't / wasn't).
5. Q: (Is / Was) there a balcony at your new apartment?   A: Yes, there (is / was).

Read the description of Paolo's old apartment. Fill in the blanks with *was* or *were*.

My old apartment was my home for four years. It **6** _____ very big. The bedroom **7** _____ nice—I have a lot of clothes, so I **8** _____ happy that there **9** _____ two closets. There **10** _____ a home office next to the bedroom for studying, and the kitchen **11** _____ great. There **12** _____ four burners on the stove, so I could cook big meals for my friends. But my old apartment **13** _____ far from school, and there **14** _____ no subway stops nearby. Oh, and the view **15** _____ not good. The one from my new apartment is awesome.

Brief note

A *closet* is a very small room where you put clothes and other things.

F Use the Language

Talking about where you lived in the past

1. Write five questions to ask your partner about his or her old home.

_____

_____

_____

_____

_____

2. Close your book and interview your partner. Then answer your partner's questions.

A Model Conversation

Read the conversation. Then listen. 🔘 Track 42

Karina: How was your visit with Paolo?

Natalia: It was great. There was so much to do, and his apartment was beautiful.

Karina: It sounds like you had fun.

Natalia: We did. There were lots of shops and restaurants nearby, and there were a subway stop and a bank right next door. There was also a movie theater nearby with great movies. We were busy every night.

Karina: What about the mornings?

Natalia: Paola was at school, so I was free to relax and explore the neighborhood.

Karina: It sounds like you were active all week. Are there any pictures of your trip on your phone?

> **Brief note**
> "(Right) next door" means next to a building or place.

B Vocabulary

Listen to the conversation again. Put a check mark next to the words that you hear. 🔘 Track 42

| clothing store | bakery | supermarket | bank | gallery |
| gym | park | market | museum | pharmacy |

C Vocabulary Comprehension

Natalia is describing Paolo's neighborhood. Look at the map and complete the sentences.

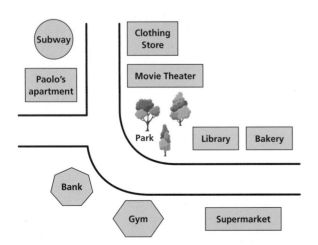

1. The movie theater was next to a _____.

2. There was a _____ next to Paolo's apartment.

3. There was a supermarket next to the _____.

4. There was a park between the _____ and the _____ _____.

5. There was a gym across from the _____.

Grammar

there was/were; conjunctions *or* and *but*

there was / there were		
There was a subway stop next door to Paolo's apartment.	**There wasn't** much noise in the apartment building.	**Was there** a library nearby?
There were many things to do in Paolo's neighborhood.	**There weren't** any bookstores nearby.	**Were there** stores in the area?
using *or*		using *but*
There wasn't a bookstore **or** a school in Paolo's neighborhood.		There was a restaurant, **but** there wasn't a coffee shop.
There weren't any churches **or** museums.		There weren't any hospitals, **but** there was a dentist's office.

Grammar Practice

Natalia is writing a postcard to her friend about her visit to Paolo's. Circle the correct word to complete each sentence.

Dear Ella,

There (❶ is / are) so much to tell you! My visit with Paolo was wonderful. There (❷ was / were) so much to do while I was there.

His neighborhood (❸ was / were) very nice. There (❹ was / were) a park across the street, and there (❺ are / were) shops nearby. There (❻ is / were) always fun things to do.

There (❼ was / were) a gym down the street, (❽ but / or) you know me—I (❾ was / were) at the park, not the gym!

There (❿ is / are) so many photos to show you when I see you. Talk to you soon!

Natalia XO

Use the Language

Describing a place

Think about a place you visited when you were younger. What do you remember? What things were there?

Find a partner. Describe the place.

Ask your partner questions about his or her memories. Then answer your partner's questions.

A Authentic Text: A movie schedule

Listen to the conversation. Then read the movie schedule. Track 43

Now playing at Rialto Cinema

Monday–Sunday this week

Theater 1   I'll See You Someday
1 p.m.   5 p.m.   7:30 p.m.   10 p.m. (Saturday only)

Theater 2   Never on a Tuesday
2 p.m.   7 p.m.   9:30 p.m.

Theater 3   Scary Monster II
4 p.m.   9 p.m.   11:30 p.m. (Friday and Saturday only)
Horror—no children under 18.

Theater 4   Dance Dance Dance
11:30 a.m.   2 p.m.   5:30 p.m.   7 p.m.
Comedy for the whole family.

Ticket prices: Adults—$10 / Children 12 and under—$7   *Tuesday:* All tickets—$5

Which movies are good choices for Paolo and Natalia?

Which movies are most interesting to you?

Brief note

When giving ages in English, we often just say the number without saying "years old." What ages do you see in the movie schedule?

B Vocabulary

Listen to the conversation again. Put a check mark next to the words that you hear. Track 43

in the morning

in the afternoon

in the evening

at night

on the weekend

Brief note

Evening is the time between sunset and bedtime.

on Monday, Tuesday, etc.

in January, February, etc.

at 2 o'clock

at 10:35

C Comprehension

Look at the schedule in part A and answer the questions.

1. Which movie plays at 11:30 p.m.?   _____

2. Which movie plays the earliest?   _____

3. Which movie is good for young children?   _____

4. Which movie is playing in Theater 2?   _____

5. How many evening shows are there?   _____

D In Your World

Answer the questions with a time expression. Find a partner and ask him or her the questions.

When do you...	You	Your partner
...watch TV?		
...study?		
...go on vacation?		
...celebrate your birthday?		

E Grammar

Prepositions with time expressions (*in / on / at*)

in	*on*	*at*
the morning / the afternoon / the evening January, February, March, etc. spring, summer, fall, winter	the weekend Sunday, Monday, Tuesday, etc. a specific date (May 4th, July 7th)	noon midnight night 6:00, 7:30, etc.
examples		
I drink coffee **in** the morning. My best friend is coming to visit **on** the weekend. The store closes **at** 6:30 p.m.	My birthday is **in** January. He was here **on** Sunday. She was born **at** 7:34 a.m.	

F Grammar Practice

Fill in the blanks with *in*, *on*, or *at*.

a. ____ Friday   b. ____ January 1st c. ____ April   d. ____ spring   e. ____ noon

f. ____ 9:30 a.m. g. ____ summer   h. ____ December i. ____ August 4th j. ____ Tuesday morning

G Use the Language

Daily routines

1. What is your daily routine—what do you do? When? Where? Make notes about your routine in the box.

2. Find a partner. Close your book. Ask your partner questions about his or her daily routine. Then answer your partner's questions.

A Model Conversation

Read the conversation. Then listen. 🔊 Track 44

Anna: Hey, Paolo. How was your weekend?

Paolo: It was great. How about yours?

Anna: Not bad. I looked after my friend's son on Saturday. He's a good kid, but he acted up a lot. I looked up lots of activities on the Internet to try and keep him busy.

Paolo: That sounds stressful. I dropped Natalia off at the airport on Saturday. Then I just listened to music on the balcony and went to bed early. I relaxed all day Sunday, too.

Anna: That sounds nice. On Sunday I wanted to do something relaxing, too, so I called up some friends to go dancing.

Paolo: That sounds like fun!

B Vocabulary

Read the conversation again. Write *A* next to the activities that Anna did and *P* next to the ones that Paolo did. Put an *X* next to activities Anna and Paolo did not do. Then match the expressions to the correct definitions.

1. _____ look after •
2. _____ act up •
3. _____ look up •
4. _____ drop (someone) off •
5. _____ kick (someone) out •
6. _____ look in on •

   • **a.** to remove (someone) from a place because of bad behavior
   • **b.** to find information
   • **c.** to take care of
   • **d.** to behave badly
   • **e.** to check whether someone is okay
   • **f.** to drive (someone) to a place and leave him or her there

C Vocabulary Comprehension

Fill in the blanks with the correct forms of the phrases from part B.

1. The teacher _____ _____ students who don't listen in class.

2. My mother always _____ _____ on my brother when he is doing homework.

3. My dog never _____ _____ when we go to the park.

4. My mother _____ me _____ at school on her way to work.

5. I use the dictionary to _____ _____ words I don't know.

6. My best friend _____ _____ her litter sister on the weekends.

Grammar

Simple past (regular verbs) and past time expressions

simple past (regular verbs): verb + -ed		
statements	**negatives**	**yes/no questions**
I He / She / It **watched** TV. We / You / They	I He / She / It **did not watch** TV. We / You / They **(didn't)**	I **Did** he / she / it **watch** TV? we / you / they
past time expressions		
yesterday last week(end) / month / year last Friday two days / weeks / months / years ago		

Brief note

Except for the verb *be* (see Lesson 1 of this unit), in the simple past, verb forms are the same for all subjects.

E **Grammar Practice**

Make sentences using an item from each column. Change the verbs to the simple past.

subject	verb	past time expression
Rinaldo Jacques and Helen My sister	cook dinner in the kitchen watch a movie in the living room clean the bathroom listen to the radio in the bedroom call his/her mother	yesterday last Monday three days ago last night two weeks ago

1. _____

2. _____

3. _____

4. _____

5. _____

F **Use the Language**

When did you do…?

Find a partner.

Ask your partner questions using past time expressions. Make notes about his or her answers in the box.

Find out what your partner did…

    yesterday
    three days ago
    last night
    last weekend
    last year

Share your partner's answers with the class.

A — Authentic Text: A planner entry

Read the schedule. Then listen to the monologue. 🔊 Track 45

Daily Routine

- 6:00 — wake up
- 6:15 — take a shower
- 6:30 — eat breakfast
- 6:45 — drink coffee & read news
- 7:30 — leave for school
- 7:45 — get on the subway
- 8:15 — get to school
- 12:00 — have lunch
- 12:30 — go to the gym
- 5:00 — get home
- 7:00 — run in the park
- 8:30 — read a book
- 10:00 — go to bed

Paolo: Yesterday was a typical day for me. I woke up, took a shower, and ate breakfast. I drank my coffee while reading news on the Internet, and then I left for school.

As usual, I took the subway, and I got to school around 8:15 a.m. I had lunch at noon, and then I went to the gym.

I got home around 5:00 p.m. and made dinner. After dinner I ran in the park. Then I went home and read a book. At 10:00, I went to bed.

Brief note

"Typical" means usual.

B — Vocabulary

Read Paolo's daily routine. Write *a.m.* next to the things he did in the morning and *p.m.* next to the things he did in the afternoon and evening. Then listen and repeat. 🔊 Track 46

got home ___

ran ___

ate breakfast ___

drank coffee ___

woke up ___

went to the gym ___

had lunch ___

took the subway ___

left for school ___

made dinner ___

read news ___

C — In Your World

Write what you did yesterday. Then ask a partner what he or she did and write the answers.

What did you do...	You	Your partner
...yesterday morning?		
...yesterday afternoon?		
...last night?		

D Grammar

Simple past (irregular verbs)

Brief note

The spelling of *read* is the same for the present and past tenses, but the past tense form is pronounced like *red*.

simple past: some irregular verbs		examples	
wake – woke leave – left drink – drank read – read go – went make – made	think – thought teach – taught have – had eat – ate get – got take – took	statement	I **ate** breakfast.
		negative	They **did not (didn't) eat** breakfast.
		question	**Did** she **eat** breakfast?

E Grammar Practice

Fill in the blanks with the simple past forms of the verbs.

David: Paolo, ① _____ you _____ (do) anything interesting yesterday?

Paolo: Not really. I ② _____ _____ (wake up) at the usual time and ③ _____ (go) to school.

David: ④ _____ you _____ (go) to the gym?

Paolo: No, I ⑤ _____ (go). I ⑥ _____ (be) too tired. What ⑦ _____ you _____ (do)?

David: I ⑧ _____ (have) lunch with my brother and ⑨ _____ (go) home early.

Paolo: Sounds like a relaxing day.

F Quick Review

Look back at the brief notes in this module.

1. What word or phrase means... *usual*? _____ *not late*? _____

2. An informal way of saying *a lot of* is _____ _____.

G Use the Language

What did you do last week?

Fill in the chart with things that you did last week. Then find a partner. Use the chart to tell your partner about the things you did.

Your activities last week	Monday	Tuesday	Wednesday	Thursday	Friday	Saturday	Sunday
morning							
afternoon							
evening							

Active Review

A Janet's Old Apartment

Listen to Janet talk about her old apartment. Fill in the blanks with the missing words. ⏺ Track 47

Nathan: Hey, Janet. What's up?

Janet: I'm thinking about my old _____. It _____ the best.

Nathan: Tell me about it.

Janet: Well, it was across from the _____ _____, so it was easy to get to _____. It _____ two _____, with a home _____ and a very big _____.

Nathan: _____ it expensive?

Janet: A little. But it was across from shops and _____, and my _____ was nearby. It only took five minutes to walk to the _____, so I _____ there every day.

Nathan: Wow. So what happened? Why _____ you move?

Janet: I _____ a dog, and the building _____ dog-friendly.

Nathan: That's too bad.

Practice the conversation with a partner. Then switch roles and practice again.

> **Brief note**
> A *dog-friendly* building is a building you can take dogs inside.

B Your Old Apartment

Search the Internet for an apartment that you would like to live in. Imagine that you lived there in the past. Think of some things about the apartment and the neighborhood that were great, as well as things you did when you lived there. Take notes.

> My Old Apartment

Show your picture to a partner and describe your life at your old apartment. Then ask your partner about his or hers.

C Reminder

Some Module 3 Goals in Unit 6

Put a check mark (✓) next to the things you can do.

_____ Write simple sentences about yourself (for example, where you live)

_____ Indicate time by such phrases as *last Friday*

_____ Describe your home and where you live

Write the simple past forms of the verbs.

1. have _____   **3.** walk _____   **5.** be _____ / _____   **7.** do _____
2. like _____   **4.** live _____   **6.** help _____

B	**Listen for Information**

Listen to a man describe two apartments: the one he lived in before and the one he lives in now. Take notes about each apartment. Which apartment does the man seem to like better? How do you know? 🔊 Track 48

C	**Write**

Think about one of your old houses or apartments. What was it like? What did you do there? How is it different from where you live now?

On a separate piece of paper, describe your old house or apartment and the one you live in now. Don't talk about which one you like better.

D	**Present**

Read your description to your class. Can they guess which place you like better?

A Vocabulary

Complete the crossword puzzle.

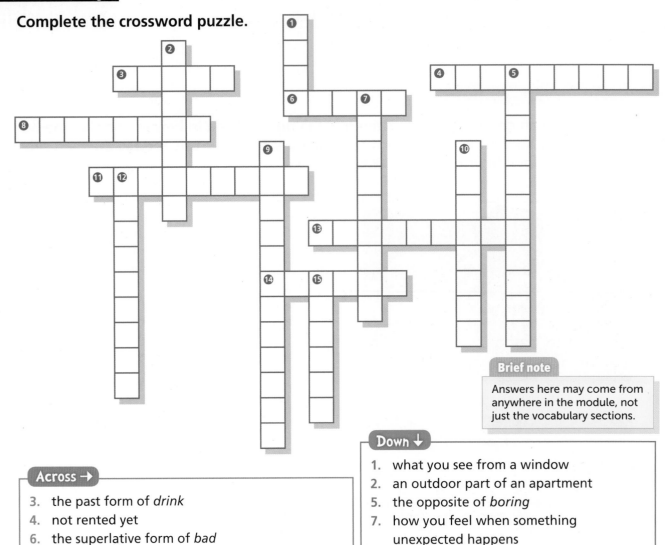

Across →

3. the past form of *drink*
4. not rented yet
6. the superlative form of *bad*
8. where you go to get medicine
11. an adjective describing a place that has furniture
13. the people who live near you
14. the comparative form of *good*

Down ↓

1. what you see from a window
2. an outdoor part of an apartment
5. the opposite of *boring*
7. how you feel when something unexpected happens
9. the area a person lives in
10. When something bothers you, say it's ___.
12. heat and lights
15. the past form of *teach*

B Grammar

Fill in the blanks with the correct forms of the given words.

I _____ (move) here three years ago to study music at the university. A year ago, I _____ (rent) a new apartment closer to the school. The new apartment is much _____ (good) than my old one. It _____ (be) not very expensive, so I _____ (be) able to save more money now. The neighbors are _____ (friendly) than my old neighbors, and there _____ (be) a lot to do in the neighborhood. I _____ (take) the bus to school last year, but after moving here, I _____ (start) to ride my bike. I _____ (need) the exercise. I _____ (be) fat, but I'm in the _____ (good) shape of my life now. I _____ (feel) good here. I _____ (have) one more year at school, and I _____ (not want) to move.

C Constructing a Conversation

Put the conversation in the correct order. The first and last sentences are already in the right place. Then listen and check. 🔘 **Track 49**

_1_ Hi, Lisa. How are you?

___ Really? That was my least favorite subject in college.

___ Sarah, hi. I'm surprised to see you here. I'm good. And you?

___ You don't look happy about that. How was it?

___ Oh, you're in school now. I forgot. What are you studying?

___ I'm studying history. It's really interesting.

___ Oh? What did you study?

___ That sounds easy, then. Actually, I had French class earlier today.

___ I'm not. For me, French is really confusing.

___ French. My mother is French, so I already spoke it pretty well.

___ Not bad. A little tired. I'm working really hard at school.

_12_ Then maybe I can help you.

D Dream Homes

Imagine your dream home (the place you would most like to live; the perfect home for you). Make notes about it in the box. Include the following:

- Where it is (city, country)
- House or apartment?
- Number and type of rooms
- What is nearby
- Your typical day at home

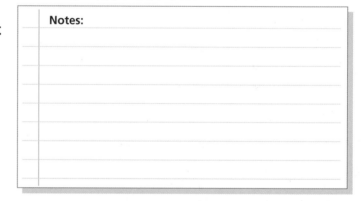

Notes:

Now find a partner. Interview your partner about his or her dream home. Ask questions about the information listed above. Then use your notes to answer your partner's questions about your dream home.

E Benjamin's Saturday

This is Benjamin. He had an interesting day last Saturday. On a separate piece of paper, write a short story (at least five sentences) about his day, using the photos below. You can choose the order and add any details you want, but <u>use all the photos in your story</u>.

In pairs or small groups, read your story. The listener(s) should try to put the photos in the right order.

Module 4 Goals

Understand short, simple messages (for example, SMS phone messages)

Find basic information in advertisements

Follow short, simple written directions

Talk about plans for one's next vacation

Ask for basic information about travel and buy tickets

Discuss plans with other people (for example, what to do and where to go)

Correctly use simple phrases you have learned for specific situations

Understand short, clear, simple messages at the airport

Preview

Look at pages 92 to 117.

On p. 93, can you identify the flags on the suitcase? Write three countries.

_____ _____ _____

What travel activities do you see in the unit? Write three activities.

_____ _____ _____

On what pages do you see travel advertisements? Write the page numbers.

_____ _____

On what page do you see people hiking? Write the page number.

_____

Write and Discuss

Write your answers to the questions. Then talk about them with a partner.

1. Do you like to travel? Why or why not?

2. What countries do you want to visit? Why?
   I want to visit ... because ...

3. What do you know about airports?
   I know they ...

4. What do you bring with you when you travel?

5. What is your plan for the week? Are you usually busy?

Unit 7

Unit 8

Scan the QR code to watch a preview video.

| Lesson 1 | **Thinking About a Trip** |

A Model Conversation

Read the conversation. Then listen. 🔘 Track 50

Cathy: Wow, look at this picture. My friend is traveling in Asia right now. I want to go on a trip.

Max: Me too. That looks amazing. Where do you want to go?

Cathy: Hmm. I want to go somewhere off the beaten path.

Max: I do too. Let's check online for some exciting tours.

Cathy: Great idea. Oh, take a look at this. How about riding a camel in the desert in Morocco?

Max: Uh, I don't know... What about exploring the jungles of Costa Rica?

Cathy: That sounds cool, too. There are a lot of options for thrill-seekers like us.

> **Brief note**
> "Me too" and "I do too" show that you agree with someone. See Lesson 2 to learn more.

B Vocabulary

Study the words and phrases. Then practice with a partner.

| check online | camel | Morocco | desert | jungle |

Match the expressions to the correct definitions.

1. thrill-seeker •   • **a.** a trip through a new place
2. explore •   • **b.** one of two or more choices
3. off the beaten path •   • **c.** a person who likes to do exciting things
4. option •   • **d.** to travel around a place to learn about it
5. tour •   • **e.** in a place where not many people go

Mexico

Costa Rica

C Vocabulary Comprehension

Fill in the blanks with the correct words and phrases from the box.

| desert | tours | camel | explore | options | jungle | off the beaten path |

1. Cathy wants to go _____ on her trip.
2. Max wants to see the _____ in Costa Rica.
3. Cathy wants to ride a(n) _____ in the desert.
4. Max is looking on the Internet for _____.
5. There is a _____ in Morocco.
6. There are a lot of _____ available to Max and Cathy.
7. Max and Cathy are thrill-seekers. They like to _____ new places.

D Grammar

Making suggestions with *let's* + verb or *What about / How about* + verb + *-ing*

making suggestions using *let's*	making suggestions with *What about / How about* + verb + *-ing*
Use *let's* + the base form of the verb.	Use *what* or *how* + *about* + the *-ing* form of the verb.
Let's check online for tours. **Let's ride** a camel in the desert.	**What about exploring** the jungles of Costa Rica? **How about going** on a tour?

Brief note

Let's is short for *Let us*, but don't say *Let us*. It's hardly ever used.

E Grammar Practice

Circle the correct answers.

1. How about (going / go) to New York in December?
2. What about (take / taking) a tour of the new university campus?
3. Let's (travel / traveling) to the jungles of Brazil.
4. What about (visiting / visit) my aunt and uncle in Egypt?
5. (Let's / Let) book a trip to Costa Rica for next summer.
6. How about (going / go) to China to see the Great Wall?

F Use the Language

Suggesting where to travel

With a partner, suggest three places to travel to:

1. _____

2. _____

3. _____

Now suggest some things that a person can do in each place, together or alone. Discuss your ideas first, and then write down some interesting points from your conversation.

Place #1	Place #2	Place #3
_____	_____	_____
_____	_____	_____
_____	_____	_____
_____	_____	_____

Work with another group. With your partner, ask what the people in the other group like to do. Then suggest that they go to one of the places you discussed above. Where should they go? Do they want to go there?

A   Model Conversation

Read the conversation. Then listen. 🔵 Track 51

Max: Okay, Cathy, where are we going to go? There are so many cool places to visit.

Cathy: Here, this ad for India looks interesting.

Max: Hmm, I don't want to go to India in the summer. It's too hot.

Cathy: Oh, good point. Me neither. I hate extreme heat.

Max: China seems exciting. My sister is traveling there next year.

Cathy: Really? Are your parents visiting her when she's there?

Max: I'm not sure. They don't like Chinese food very much.

Cathy: I don't either. It's too spicy for me.

Max: I'm having Chinese for dinner tonight—yum!

B   Vocabulary

Match the pictures to the words or phrases in the box.

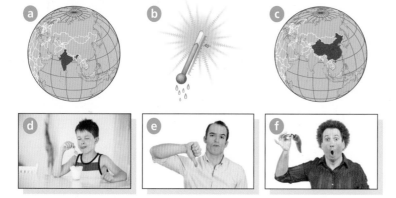

spicy	_____
extreme heat	_____
China	_____
yum	_____
hate	_____
India	_____

C   In Your World

Think about your country's weather and food. Write down what you like and what you hate. Then talk with a partner. Write down your partner's answers.

For example:

A: I hate the cold weather in the winter. How about you?

B: I love the cold, but I don't like the extreme heat in the summer.

Weather I like: _____

Weather I hate: _____

Food I love: _____

Food I don't like: _____

Weather my partner likes: _____

Weather my partner hates: _____

Food my partner loves: _____

Food my partner doesn't like: _____

Grammar

Discussing the future; showing agreement

present continuous with future meaning	agreement	
S + *be* + verb-*ing*	**with positive statements**	**with negative statements**
I am having Chinese food for dinner **tonight**. **My sister is traveling** to China **next year**.	A: I love Japanese food. B: **Me too. / I do too!**	A: I don't like spicy food. B: **Me neither. / I don't either.**

Grammar Practice

Put the words in order to make sentences.

1. Italian / I / am / dinner / for / having / tomorrow / night

   _____.

2. we / meeting / our / are / tonight / parents

   _____.

3. going / my / trip / is / on / month / next / a / friend

   _____.

4. I / this / to / am / interview / tomorrow / wearing / the

   _____.

Complete the conversations with the correct agreement phrases. Then practice with a partner.

5. **Mary:** I really love hot weather! **Joe:** _____

6. **Duncan:** I don't enjoy the winters—they get so cold! **Sophia:** _____

Use the Language

And you?

Write sentences about things you like or don't like and what you're going to do in the future. Then find three people and discuss your sentences. Write a check mark when people agree with you and an *X* when they disagree. Keep the discussion going with follow-up questions. Share your answers with the class.

Statement	Names		
	_____	_____	_____
I hate...			
I really like...			
I...			
I...			
I...			

What could we do on vacation?

A Model Conversation

Read the conversation. Then listen. `Track 52`

Cathy: Here, Max. Look at this travel ad for Peru. It's really interesting. There are so many incredible things we could do.

Max: Yeah, that looks fantastic. We could hike along the Inca Trail.

Cathy: Or we could take a train and then hike into the jungle for a real adventure!

Max: We have to visit Machu Picchu. I could spend hours there. I'm a history fan.

Cathy: I couldn't stay that long. But you're right—we have to go. We could go there and then do the jungle hike.

Max: It says here we can take a riverboat along the Amazon, too.

Cathy: I can't go. I get sick on boats.

B Vocabulary

Study the words. Then practice with a partner.

river

riverboat

hike

trail

C Vocabulary

Read the sentences. Match the underlined words to the correct definitions. One definition is used twice.

1. _____ I'm a history <u>fan</u>.
2. _____ Look at all the <u>incredible</u> things we can do.
3. _____ Yeah, that looks <u>fantastic</u>.
4. _____ I saw an <u>ad</u> in a magazine.
5. _____ We really had an <u>adventure</u> in Peru!

a. short form of the word *advertisement*
b. great; amazing
c. someone who really likes something
d. an exciting time

Now write a new sentence using each word. Then read your sentences to a partner.

ad: _____

fan: _____

fantastic: _____

incredible: _____

adventure: _____

D In Your World

Discuss these questions with a partner. Then share your answers with another pair.

What do you like to do when you travel?   What are you a fan of? Why?

E Grammar

can for ability; can and could for possibility

can for ability: can + verb	can and could for possibility: can/could + verb
Use *can* to talk about ability—things you're able to do.	Use *can* or *could* to talk about possibility in the present or the future. *Could* means the same as *can* in this context but is less direct.
I **can speak** three languages: English, Spanish, and German. She **can't swim** very well.	We **can/could hike** along the Inca Trail, or we **can/could take** the train. We **can/could go** to Machu Picchu.

F Grammar Practice

Fill in the blanks with the correct words from the box.

can	speak	can't	hike	could	eat

1. Can you _____ French, too?

2. I _____ meet you at the station. See you there.

3. I _____ swim well. Let's not go to the river.

4. When we visit China, we _____ see the Great Wall.

5. He can't _____ spicy food—it hurts his stomach.

6. We could _____ up to the top of the mountain. The views are incredible, I'm sure.

G Use the Language

Could we go together?

Look at these travel ads. Think about which place you want to visit and why.

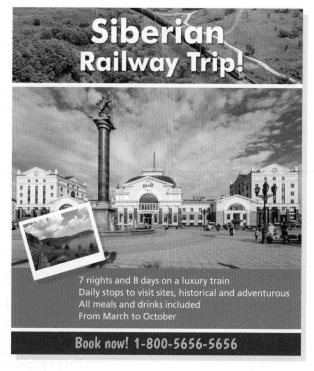

Now find a partner and ask where he or she wants to go. Talk about what you could do in each place. Do you have similar ideas? Do you want to travel together? Why or why not?

A   Authentic Text: An email exchange

Read the emails. Then listen. 🎧 Track 53

To:	Cathy M <magiccathy@mail.com>
From:	Max <madmax@mail.com>
Date:	Mon, Aug 15 at 9:21 PM
Subject:	Trip

Hi, Max.

We need to call the travel agency ASAP to book our plane tickets. I can do that tomorrow morning. I don't have class, so I can call them and then let you know. We need to decide on specific dates for our trip. What do you think?

Cathy

To:	Max <madmax@mail.com>
From:	Cathy M <magiccathy@mail.com>
Date:	Mon, Aug 15 at 10:07 PM
Subject:	Re: Trip

Hi, Cathy.

Before you call the travel agency, I can do a quick search online tonight to compare prices. We need to find the best deal possible. After checking the prices, we can decide on the dates. Oh, and do we need to pay in person, or can we pay online?

Max

Brief note

"In person" means face to face—looking at the other person involved.

B   Vocabulary

Listen to each word or phrase. Repeat. Then write the words and phrases next to the correct definitions. 🎧 Track 54

travel agency	book	compare	ASAP	deal	specific	date	quick	ticket

Definition	Word(s)
the number of the day in the month (for example, October 1st)	
to look at two or more things in order to see how they are alike or different	
a place that sells vacations	
exact; particular	
to reserve; to schedule	
fast	
"as soon as possible" = quickly; right away	
a piece of paper that lets you travel on a bus, plane, train, etc.	
a good price	

C   In Your World

Look online or in a newspaper. Find two travel ads. Use them to fill in the table.

Travel Ad #1	Travel Ad #2
Name of travel agency:	Name of travel agency:
Destination:	Destination:
Dates of travel:	Dates of travel:
Details:	Details:

Share your information with a partner.

D Grammar

can for offers and volunteering; *need to* for obligation

can for offers and volunteering S + *can* + verb	*need to* for obligation S + *need to* + verb
Use *can* to make offers or volunteer to do things.	Use *need to* like *have to* (See Unit 2 Lesson 5). Use it when you have an obligation (something you have to do).
I **can call** the travel agency tomorrow. I have some free time. I **can do** a quick search online to check prices.	We **need to call** the travel agency ASAP. It is necessary to get the tickets. Do we **need to pay** in person, or can we do it online?

Brief note

Here, *can* is used to make offers in statements. See Unit 8 Lesson 1 to learn how to use *can* to make offers in questions.

E Grammar Practice

Underline the errors and write the correct word(s) on the lines.

1. I can calling you later with more information. _____

2. She needs to remembering her passport. _____

3. Do I need bring my book? _____

4. He can doing a search on their website. _____

5. We need to booked the tickets in advance. _____

6. They needing to pack their suitcases. _____

7. Mr. Brown can buying tickets online. _____

8. My teacher can't not help us with the test. _____

9. Can I helped you? _____

10. Do we need to showing our passports? _____

F Use the Language

Planning a trip

You and a partner want to plan a vacation. Choose a destination and make a list of things that you need to do to plan the trip.

To-Do List
☐
☐
☐
☐
☐
☐
☐

Share your travel plans and list with the class. Explain why you need to do those things.

A Model Conversation

Read the conversation. Then listen. Track 55

Cathy: Okay, Max. Tell me where on the plane you want to sit.

Max: Please don't put me in a window seat. I'm afraid of heights.

Cathy: Really? Okay, it says, "Click here to reserve." Done.

Max: Don't close the window. It's still processing.

Cathy: Now it says, "Choose ticket type." Do we want to print our tickets, or do we want e-tickets?

Max: Don't print them. We can just bring our passports to the airport. They match the passport to the ticket number.

Cathy: Then don't forget to bring your passport.

Max: Of course. That's the most important thing.

B Vocabulary

Read each word or phrase, listen, and repeat. Then match each word or phrase to the correct picture. Track 56

afraid of heights ( )   click ( )   airport ( )   print ( )   passport ( )

C Vocabulary: On an airplane

Read. Then listen and practice. Track 57

window seat

overhead compartment

aisle seat

middle seat

aisle

Can you think of words for other parts of the airplane? Write them below. Then draw arrows to match them to the picture.

_____   _____   _____   _____   _____

D In Your World

Discuss these questions with a partner. Then share your answers with another pair.

Do you have experience traveling by airplane?   Do/Would you like to fly? Why or why not?

On an airplane, where do you like to sit?   What do you think about traveling by air?

Grammar

Imperatives

Use imperatives to give commands, make suggestions, give instructions, or encourage someone.			
affirmative imperatives: verb (base form)		**negative imperatives: *Do not / Don't* + verb**	
Take care.	(suggestion/farewell)	**Don't forget** your passport.	(command)
Be on time, please.	(command/instruction)	**Don't close** the window.	(instruction)
Tell me where you want		**Don't put** me in a window seat.	(command)
to sit on the plane.	(command)	**Don't work** too hard.	(suggestion/farewell)
Click here to save.	(instruction)	**Don't give up**.	(encouragement)

Grammar Practice

Fill in the blanks with words from part E.

1. _____ forget to pack a bathing suit. There's a beautiful pool at the hotel.

2. _____ here to book your trip online.

3. Have a great trip. _____ care!

4. _____ faster. You need to finish this work quickly.

5. Don't _____ the window yet. I need to type my passport number.

6. _____ your bag in the overhead compartment.

7. The plane leaves at 6:15. _____ be late!

8. _____ us about your trip. Was it fun?

Write to Speak

Make a list of suggestions using imperatives. Suggest what a friend should do for his or her next trip. Then share your ideas with a partner.

1. _____.

2. _____.

3. _____.

4. _____.

Use the Language

Talking to a travel agent

Role-play a conversation between a travel agent and a customer.

Travel Agent: Help your customer book a trip. Answer questions about how he or she can prepare for it.

Customer: Book a trip and ask the travel agent about how to prepare for it.

After you finish, summarize your conversation with another pair.

A A Travel Flyer

Create a travel flyer for a place you want to visit.

The flyer must include:

- the name of the place
- a picture of the place
- things you can do there
- things you need to bring
- how to book the trip online
- how long the trip is
- prices and options
- contact information for the travel agency

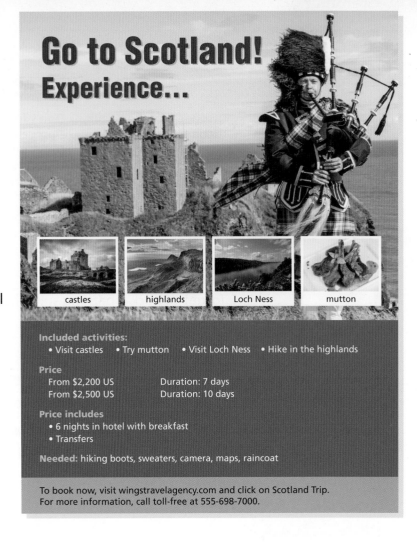

Go to Scotland!
Experience...

castles   highlands   Loch Ness   mutton

Included activities:
- Visit castles   • Try mutton   • Visit Loch Ness   • Hike in the highlands

Price
From $2,200 US   Duration: 7 days
From $2,500 US   Duration: 10 days

Price includes
- 6 nights in hotel with breakfast
- Transfers

Needed: hiking boots, sweaters, camera, maps, raincoat

To book now, visit wingstravelagency.com and click on Scotland Trip.
For more information, call toll-free at 555-698-7000.

B Present Your Flyer

After you create your flyer, present it to a partner. Answer any questions he or she has about the place and the trip. Write the questions below.

_____

_____

_____

_____

Share your flyer with the class. Vote on the best one. Consider the following:

- Which flyer has the best design?
- Which flyer has the most detail?
- How clear is the information?

C Reminder

Some Module 4 Goals in Unit 7

Put a check mark (✓) next to the things you can do.

_____ Find basic information in advertisements

_____ Ask for basic information about travel and buy tickets

_____ Discuss plans with other people (for example, what to do and where to go)

Listen for Information

Listen and fill in the blanks. Then practice the conversation with a partner. 🔊 Track 58

Travel Agent: Sunstar _____ _____. Can I help you?
Customer: Yes, hello. I want to _____ a trip somewhere. I'm a _____-_____, so...
Travel Agent: So, are you interested in an _____ _____?
Customer: What's that?
Travel Agent: An exciting tour where you can do things like _____ mountains, take _____ along beautiful rivers, ride _____ in the _____...
Customer: Wow! That sounds _____. Do you have any trips to the _____ of _____ _____?
Travel Agent: Yes, we do. But a lot of people want those tickets. You _____ _____ book soon.
Customer: Okay, _____ _____ my friend tonight to talk about the trip. _____ _____ _____ tomorrow?
Travel Agent: Yes, or _____ _____ book online. Our website is very easy to use. _____ _____ to include your _____ number when you book your ticket.
Customer: _____ _____ your web address, please.
Travel Agent: It's www.sunstar.com.
Customer: Thank you for your help.
Travel Agent: You're welcome. _____ _____.

Prepare to Speak

Listen again and write down some things you can do on an adventure tour. Then use the Internet to write down more ideas. 🔊 Track 58

Adventure Tours

When you're finished writing, take five minutes to look back through the module. Pay close attention to the part A activities, where Cathy and Max are making plans to go on a trip.

Practice Speaking

Find a partner. Role-play a conversation between two friends planning to go on an adventure tour. Discuss these details:

What kinds of things do you want to do? Where do you want to go?

What does your friend think about it? What does he or she want to do on an adventure tour?

Now Speak

Stand up in front of the class with your partner. Role-play your conversation. After all the pairs finish, discuss these questions:

A. Which pairs were fast? Did they make many mistakes?

B. Which pairs didn't make many mistakes? Were they fast?

Lesson 1 — Going to Catch a Plane

A Model Conversation

Read the conversation. Then listen. 🔊 Track 59

Max: I don't see the check-in counter for SkyAir. Are we in the right terminal?

Cathy: Yes, this is the international terminal. Can you please get a baggage cart?

Max: Sure.

Cathy: Okay. Now where do we check in?

Man: You look lost. Can I help you find something?

Cathy: Yes, could you tell me where the SkyAir check-in counter is?

Man: Sure. Go through these doors and then to the right. It's past the escalator.

Cathy: Thank you!

Max: Okay, here you are. Let's go—I don't want to be late. Wow, Cathy, you brought a lot of luggage with you!

B Vocabulary

Study the words and phrases. Then practice with a partner.

baggage cart

check in

check-in counter

gate

terminal

escalator

lost

late

C Vocabulary Comprehension

Write the words from part B next to the correct definitions.

1. one large part of an airport   _____
2. a moving staircase   _____
3. a place to get your tickets and boarding pass   _____
4. a place where you get on the airplane   _____
5. not knowing where you are   _____
6. not on time   _____
7. something to help you move luggage   _____
8. to get your tickets and boarding pass   _____

can and *could* for offers and requests

can for offers		*can/could* for requests
Can I + verb...? / I can + verb		**Can/Could + S + verb...?**
Can I help you find something? **I can help you** find something.		**Can/Could you tell** me where the check-in counter is? A: **Can/Could I** use your pen, please? B: Sure, here you are.

E **Grammar Practice**

Put the words in order to make sentences.

1. I / help / you / something / can / find

   _____?

2. you / hold / could / my / ticket

   _____?

3. can / get / baggage cart / you / a

   _____?

4. sure, / here / are / you

   _____.

5. close / you / could / door, / the / please

   _____?

F **Listen to Write**

Read the conversation between two friends at an airport gate. Then listen. Underline the requests and offers. Write *R* by the requests and *O* by the offers. Compare your answers with a partner. 🔊 Track 60

Man:	We have an hour before our plane leaves. That's a lot of time. Are you hungry?
Woman:	No, I'm not, but I'd love some coffee.
Man:	Me, too. Good idea. I can go to the coffee shop. Could you stay here with the luggage?
Woman:	Yeah, no problem. Could you get a large coffee for me? I can give you some money—just a second...
Man:	No, that's okay. I can pay.
Woman:	All right. I can't find my money anyway. Oh—can you please get sugar, too?
Man:	Sure.

G **Use the Language**

Offers and requests

With your partner, choose one of the following situations and write a short conversation using *can/could* for offers and requests. Perform your conversation for the class.

- Two friends at a movie theater
- A waiter/waitress and a customer
- A travel agent and a customer

A Model Conversation

Read the conversation. Then listen. 🔊 Track 61

Agent: Welcome to SkyAir. Where are you traveling today?
Max: Hi. Costa Rica. Cathy, can you **pass** my backpack to me?
Cathy: Sure. Here you go.
Agent: Tickets and passports, please.
Max: Here you are. And we have two bags to **check**.
Agent: Okay. Do you mind putting your bags on the **scale**, please?
Max: Sure. Wow, this bag is **heavy**.
Agent: Whose **suitcase** is this?
Cathy: That's mine. The gray one is his.
Agent: And whose is that over there?
Cathy: That's my **carry-on**.
Agent: All right. Here are your **boarding passes**. Enjoy your **flight**.

> **Brief note**
> "Here you go" is a less formal way of saying *Here you are*.

> **Brief note**
> "Do you mind -ing...?" is a polite way of making a request. Use *can* or the imperative with friends and family.

B Vocabulary

Look at the bold words in the conversation. Write each word next to the correct definition.

Definition	Word(s)
a trip on a plane	
a machine used to find out the weight of something	
a large piece of luggage	
difficult to lift or move	
to give (something) to another person	
pieces of paper that you show before boarding (getting on) a plane	
a small bag to take on the airplane with you	
to give (a bag, suitcase, etc.) to an employee so that they can put it on the plane	

C Vocabulary Comprehension

Fill in the blanks in the conversations below with the correct words from part B. Listen and check. Then match each conversation with the correct picture. 🔊 Track 62

1. A: Can I see your passport and _____
   _____, please?
   B: Sure. Here you are.

2. A: Are you taking much luggage?
   B: No, just a small bag. It's a _____.

3. A: Can I help you with that suitcase?
   B: No, thanks. It's big, but it isn't
   _____.

4. A: I'd like to _____ this bag.
   B: Okay. Please put it on the scale.

A _____

B _____

C _____

D _____

Questions with *whose* and possessive pronouns

questions with *whose*	possessive pronouns
Whose + noun...?	**Possessive pronouns** replace names or a possessive adj. + noun. They describe ownership.
Whose bag is this? **Whose car** are we taking? **Whose suitcases** are these?	It's Henry's. → It's **his**. Let's take your car. → Let's take **yours**. They're my suitcases. → They're **mine**.

E **Grammar Practice**

Circle the correct answers.

1. The pink backpack is his, not (my / mine).
2. (Who's / Whose) luggage is in the car?
3. Those tickets aren't yours. They're (ours / our).
4. Roberto is looking for his phone. Is this (his / him)?
5. I have my boarding pass. Where is (your / yours)?
6. Our flight leaves at 10 o'clock, and (they / theirs) leaves at 12.

F **Quick Review**

Look back at the brief notes in this module and fill in the blanks.

1. Don't say _____ _____. Say *let's*.
2. The phrase *face to face* means _____ _____.
3. When you give something to someone, say _____ _____ _____
   or _____ _____ _____.

G **Use the Language**

Let's pack!

Imagine you and a friend are packing your suitcases for a vacation. Think about where you are going and how long you are going for.

Now role-play the situation. Request that your partner pass you things to add to your suitcase, and help your partner. Identify which things are yours and which are not. Use the items in the photos or your own ideas.

Present your conversation to the class.

A Model Conversation

Read the conversation. Then listen. 🔘 Track 63

Guard: ID and boarding passes, please.

Max: This is mine, and this one is hers.

Guard: Okay. Please place your bags on the conveyor belt and put your shoes in a bin. Then walk through the metal detector. Can you come through one more time, sir? More slowly this time, please.

Cathy: Max, you're walking too fast!

Max: Sorry, I'm a little anxious. We need to board our flight soon.

Guard: That's fine, sir. Ma'am, please come through now.

Cathy: Okay. Oh, Max—this is taking longer than I thought. I hope we still have time to go to the duty-free shop. I'm excited to see what they have!

B Vocabulary

Listen to the words or phrases. Then write them under the correct pictures. 🔘 Track 64

| bin | conveyor belt | metal detector | duty-free shop |

_____ _____ _____ _____

Match the words to the correct definitions.

1. anxious •
2. excited •
3. stressed •
4. terrified •

• a. very happy about something that is going to happen
• b. worried; nervous
• c. feeling pressure to do something in a situation
• d. very scared

C Vocabulary: The meanings of *pass*

You learned the word *pass* in Lesson 2. It also appears as part of other vocabulary words and phrases in this module: *passport* and *boarding pass*. The word *pass* has several different meanings. Read the definitions. On a separate sheet of paper, write a sentence for each definition. Then share your sentences with a partner.

> **pass¹** /pæs/ *noun*
> a paper or card that lets you enter a place (an airplane, a building, etc.): *I ride the bus often, so I have a bus **pass**.*
>
> **pass²** /pæs/ *verb*
> 1. to move past (someone or something): *We **pass** the bakery every day when we walk to school.*
> 2. to make a good enough grade; to finish (a class or exam) successfully: *Did you **pass** your history test?*

Grammar

Comparing with adverbs

adverbs	
Adverbs describe actions. They describe how the action is done and how often. Adverbs often come after the verb in the sentence: *He walked **slowly** through security.* Many adverbs are made by adding *-ly* to an adjective. To form the comparative of an *-ly* adverb, use *more* + adverb. But some words are the same in both adjective and adverb form *(early, fast).* Their comparative adverb forms are the same as their comparative adjective forms (see Unit 5 Lesson 1). Other adverbs are irregular *(well, badly, far).*	

adverbs	comparative adverbs
quietly	**more** quietly (than)
slowly	**more** slowly (than) / slow**er** (than)*
quickly	**more** quickly (than) / quick**er** (than)*
loudly	**more** loudly (than) / loud**er** (than)*
early	earl**ier** (than)
fast	fast**er** (than)
well	**better** (than)
badly	**worse** (than)
far	**farther** (than)
Quick and *slow* are sometimes used as adverbs.	

E **Grammar Practice**

Read the sentences. Fill in the blanks with the correct forms of the adverbs.

1. We arrived _____ (early) than they did.
2. She went through security _____ (fast) than the rest of the group.
3. I walk _____ (slowly) than he does.
4. He got to the airport _____ (quickly) than I did.
5. They packed their suitcases _____ (well) than they did on the last trip.
6. This conveyor belt works _____ (badly) than the other one.

F **Use the Language**

Things you can't take on the plane

Go online and find information about what you can and cannot take through the security check at your nearest airport. Make a list and share it with your partner. Are you surprised by anything?

Things you can bring:	Things you cannot bring:
_____	_____
_____	_____
_____	_____
_____	_____
_____	_____
_____	_____
_____	_____

A   Authentic Text: An airline's website

Read the information on SkyAir's website. Then listen. 🔊 Track 65

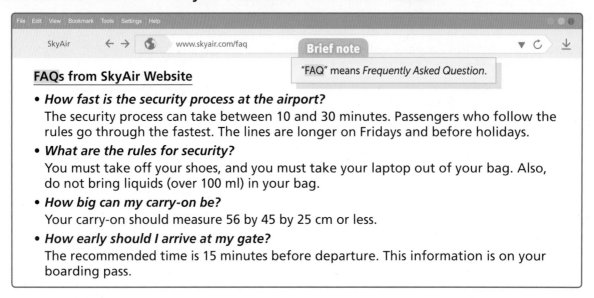

FAQs from SkyAir Website

Brief note
"FAQ" means *Frequently Asked Question*.

- *How fast is the security process at the airport?*
  The security process can take between 10 and 30 minutes. Passengers who follow the rules go through the fastest. The lines are longer on Fridays and before holidays.
- *What are the rules for security?*
  You must take off your shoes, and you must take your laptop out of your bag. Also, do not bring liquids (over 100 ml) in your bag.
- *How big can my carry-on be?*
  Your carry-on should measure 56 by 45 by 25 cm or less.
- *How early should I arrive at my gate?*
  The recommended time is 15 minutes before departure. This information is on your boarding pass.

B   Vocabulary

Listen to each word. Then write the words next to the correct definitions. 🔊 Track 66

follow	liquid	line	passenger	process	measure	departure

Definition	Word
the act of leaving	
to obey (a rule)	
a group of people waiting for something, with each person standing behind another	
a series of actions to produce a result	
something like water that you can drink or pour	
to be a certain size	
a person who rides (in an airplane, a bus, a car, etc.)	

C   Vocabulary: Measurements

Write the words from the box next to the correct short form.

liter	millimeter	centimeter	kilometer	meter

ml = _____   l = _____   cm = _____

m = _____   km = _____

D   In Your World

Go online and visit your local airport's website. Do they have an FAQ page? What questions are listed there? Do you see any mistakes on it? Take notes on the questions you see, as well as any mistakes. Did you learn anything new about air travel in your country? Share your thoughts with a partner.

E Grammar

Superlative adverbs; *how* + adverb

superlative adverbs	
To form the superlative of an *-ly* adverb, use *the most* + adverb. Adverbs with irregular comparative forms also have irregular superlative forms. (See Lesson 3 of this unit.)	

adverbs	superlative adverbs
quietly	the **most** quietly
slowly	the **most** slowly / the slo**west**
quickly	the **most** quickly / the quick**est**
early	the earli**est**
fast	the fast**est**
well	the **best**
badly	the **worst**
far	the **farthest**

how + adverbs
Like with adjectives (see Unit 1 Lesson 2), you can use *how* + adverb to ask about the degree of an adverb.
How early should I arrive at my gate? **How far** did you travel? **How fast** does she run? **How quickly** can you pack?

Brief note

The use of *quick* and *slow* as adverbs is informal.
I worked the quickest / the slowest. (informal)
I worked the most quickly / the most slowly. (formal)

F Grammar Practice

Fill in the blanks with the correct words and phrases from the box. Then read the sentences out loud.

> the fastest   the best   the earliest   fast   far   quietly   how   the worst   the slowest

1. Planes go really _____—more than 600 kilometers per hour.

2. We're late, so Max should drive. He drives _____.

3. I always get up _____—at 5 a.m.!

4. How _____ into the jungle did you go?

5. Please talk _____. My grandfather is sleeping.

6. _____ well can you speak Spanish?

7. I ski _____ out of all my friends. I don't want to go skiing on vacation!

8. Liam is good at math. He always does _____ in our class on tests.

9. My teacher says I don't work fast enough. I'm _____ in my class.

G Use the Language

I have some questions…

Imagine you are traveling to a new country. You want some information about traveling there. On a separate sheet of paper, write five questions about your trip. They can be about the airport, the hotel, things to see and do, etc.

Give your questions to a partner. Your partner should go online, find the answers to your questions, write them down, and give them back to you. Using the answers, tell your class about your trip.

A   Model Conversation

Read the conversation. Then listen. Track 67

Cathy: Our gate is over there. Our flight leaves soon.

Max: Um, I'm not sure about that. Look at the departure board—it says our flight is delayed.

Cathy: Oh, no! How long do we have to wait?

Max: It says it leaves in an hour.

Cathy: Oh, well. I have these magazines from the duty-free shop to flip through.

Max: What are you going to read on the plane?

Cathy: I have some movies to watch on my tablet.

Max: I don't have anything to do on the plane. Can I borrow your magazines later?

Cathy: Sure, if you're interested in celebrity gossip!

✈ Departures			
Time	To	Gate	Remark
15:00	LONDON	A10	CANCELLED
15:02	MADRID	A03	ON TIME
15:08	NEW YORK	A17	ON TIME
15:09	MIAMI	B15	ON TIME
15:12	COSTA RICA	B09	DELAYED
15:14	PARIS	B05	CANCELLED
15:30	BANGKOK	A12	CANCELLED
15:31	TOKYO	B01	DELAYED

B   Vocabulary

Match the expressions to the correct definitions.

1. delayed
2. magazine
3. flip through
4. celebrity
5. gossip
6. departure board

a. a board showing when planes leave
b. interesting news about other people (sometimes not true)
c. a famous person
d. not leaving on time; late
e. a small book with pictures and articles
f. read something casually or quickly

Fill in the blanks with the correct words and phrases from the box.

gossip	magazines	flip through	celebrity	delayed	departure board

7. I'm interested in _____ news—I like to read _____!
8. Look at the _____ _____. It says our flight is _____.
9. I have these _____ to _____ _____.

B   Vocabulary: Time expressions

Time expressions say when something happens (or happened) in the past, present, or future.		
Past	Present	Future
yesterday last week a few days ago last night	on Saturdays at 1.00 p.m. now between 6 and 7 p.m.	tomorrow next week in an hour / in 20 minutes soon
We saw a movie **last night**.	She works **on Saturdays**.	Our flight leaves **in an hour**.

D   In Your World

Imagine your flight is delayed. What do you want to do while you wait? Visit the duty-free shop? Read magazines? Go online and find out what people can do in your local airport. Take notes on a separate piece of paper. Then share the information with a partner.

E Grammar

have + O + to verb

have + O	have to + verb	have + O + to verb
Use *have* + O to talk about an object that you possess.	Use *have to* + verb to talk about something that is important to do.	Use *have* + O + *to* verb to talk about things that you have and that you can do or use.
I **have a pet.**	I **have to do** this homework.	I **have** these **magazines to flip through.**

F Grammar Practice

Match the first part to the second part of the sentence. Then read each one out loud to a partner.

1. The passenger has movies to   •   • a. to read on vacation.
2. She has a lot of books   •   • b. pack before he leaves.
3. I have to   •   • c. a sister and a brother.
4. They have homework   •   • d. to do tonight.
5. He has bags to   •   • e. watch on the plane.
6. I have   •   • f. call my boyfriend tonight.
7. They have a guide   •   • g. to help them on their trip.

Put the words in order to make sentences.

8. have / we / tickets / our / soon / to / book

   _____.

9. play / kids / the / to / new / game / have / a

   _____.

10. has / Gary / airport / to / go / now / the / to

   _____.

11. hungry, / have / but / eat / to / I / nothing / I'm

   _____.

12. pencil / have / my / backpack / in / I / a

   _____.

G Use the Language

A trip down memory lane

Think about a trip you took in the past. What did you do and when? Now think about a trip you want to take in the future. What do you want to do and when? What do you want to do differently? Tell your partner about both trips. Share your stories with the class. Then write a short plan for your future trip.

A Airport Information

Read the conversation and fill in the blanks with the correct words from the box. Then listen and check your answers. Practice the conversation with a partner. 🔊 Track 68

check in	how early	could	faster	mind	metal detector	gate
suitcases	more	departure board	flight	carry-on	terminal	train

Airline agent: SkyAir. Can I help you?

Traveler: Hello, I'm traveling to China tomorrow. _____ _____ do I need to arrive at the airport?

Airline agent: You should _____ _____ two hours before your flight leaves.

Traveler: Okay. _____ you tell me where the check-in counter for SkyAir is?

Airline agent: We are in _____ 3.

Traveler: Do you _____ telling me how many bags I can check?

Airline agent: Sure. You can check two _____. And one _____ is allowed. This information is also available on our website's FAQ.

Traveler: Great. What about security? Could you tell me how to pass through it _____ smoothly?

Airline agent: Be ready for the _____ _____—remove all metal objects from your pockets.

Traveler: Right.

Airline agent: Then you can take the terminal _____ to the _____. It's _____ than waiting for the bus. And don't forget to check the _____ _____ in case your _____ is delayed.

Traveler: Thank you very much for your help.

B Call the Airport

With a partner, research the nearest airport. Use what you learn to create your own conversation like the one above. Take some time to reread the conversation and replace the following information with your own.

Where are you going?   *What airline are you taking?*
What terminal is it in?   *How many bags can you check?*

Choose roles and practice with your partner. Then present your conversation to the class.

> **Brief note**
> An *airline* is a company that owns airplanes to carry passengers and other things.

C Reminder

Some Module 4 Goals in Unit 8

Put a check mark (✓) next to the things you can do.

_____ Follow short, simple written directions

_____ Understand short, clear, simple messages at the airport

_____ Correctly use simple phrases you have learned for specific situations

Warm Up

Put the letters in order to make words.

1. egta _____
2. pedurtaer _____
3. rcopses _____

4. lftgih _____
5. claes _____
6. retoclasa _____

Brainstorm

Look at the image. Discuss the symbols with a partner or your teacher. Then label them with the name of an airport place or process.

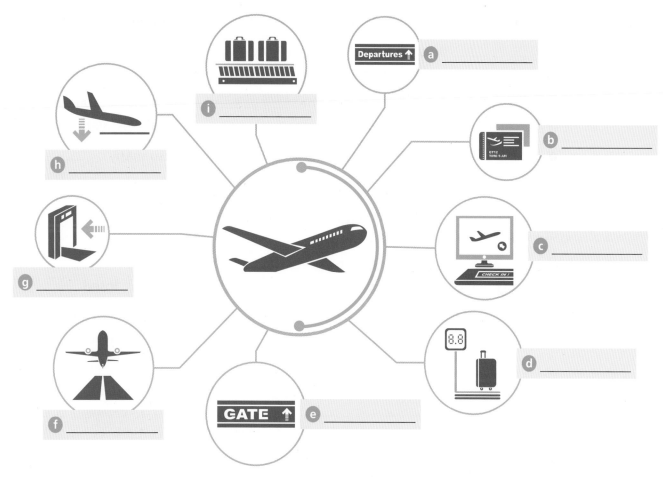

After labeling each symbol, think of questions you can ask about each image at the airport. Write your questions down on a separate piece of paper. Then share them with a partner. Your partner should write down the answers to your questions.

Write

Imagine you have a friend who never travels. He or she does not know anything about the process of going through an airport. On a separate piece of paper, design a diagram showing the process from beginning to end. Write each step and, where possible, include the letter of the image from above that matches the step.

For example,

Arrive early at the airport. → Find the check-in counter. → _____.

Share your diagram with a partner. Ask your partner's opinion—did you forget anything?

A Vocabulary

Choose the correct answers.

1. Please put your bags on the _____ and show me your _____.
   a. carry-on belt, board pass   b. convey belt, ticket pass   c. conveyor belt, boarding pass

2. People who go on _____ are _____.
   a. trails, thrill-seekers   b. adventure tours, thrill-seekers   c. riverboats, afraid of heights

3. We need to show the agent our _____ and _____.
   a. passes, tickets   b. passports, tickets   c. passports, ads

4. Your _____ should _____ 56 by 45 by 25 centimeters.
   a. carry-on, measure   b. check-in, measure   c. extreme heat, hate

5. This bag is so _____! Let's take the _____ and not the stairs.
   a. heavy, escalate   b. heavy, escalator   c. heavy, escalation

6. I am _____ of the security _____—there are so many _____ to _____!
   a. terrible, process, rules, follow
   b. terrified, processing, rules, following
   c. terrified, process, rules, follow

7. Are you _____ about getting _____ at the airport?
   a. anxious, lost   b. anxiety, lost   c. anxious, losed

8. The _____ shows our flight is _____.
   a. advertisement, delayed   b. departure board, delayed   c. gate, delayed

9. I like to read _____ on a _____.
   a. magazines, flight   b. passports, flight   c. advertisements, fly

B Grammar

Fill in the blanks with the missing word or words.

1. I _____ having dinner with my parents tonight.

2. _____ you pass my bag, please?

3. _____ forget to book the tickets online.

4. _____ care!

5. A: Is this bag yours?
   B: Yes, it's _____.

6. He walks _____ slowly than her. He's too slow.

7. I _____ a new book _____ read on the plane.

8. A: _____ suitcase is this?
   B: It's his.

9. We _____ _____ bring our passports.

10. _____ I help you?

11. Do _____ _____ holding this for a moment?

12. _____ well do you know this airport?

13. He _____ two cats and a dog at home.

14. I sing badly, but she sings worse _____ me!

15. _____ I borrow your tablet, please?

16. We arrived _____ than them.

C Planning to Travel

Plan a trip with a partner. Decide where you want to go—what country, for example—and when. Make lists of things you need to bring, things you want to bring, things you can do there, things you want to do there, and places you want to visit.

Then prepare a presentation to give to the class. Create a poster about your trip for the presentation. Include:

- The destination, dates of travel, and cost of the tickets
- A list of things to pack in your suitcases
- A list of things to do and places to go in the area
- Any other information you think is important or interesting
- If possible, pictures of where you want to go (or show pictures on your phone)

Present your poster to the class. Explain your trip and answer any questions your classmates have.

D Airport Role-Play

You have your tickets for the trip you planned in part C. Now check in—role-play a situation at an airport between the agent at the check-in counter and a traveler going on that trip.

Role A: Check-in agent

- Ask the traveler where he or she is going, and ask to see their tickets and passports.
- Ask the traveler about his or her bags.
- Give him or her a boarding pass.

Role B: Traveler(s)

- Check in for your flight.
- Ask the agent about your boarding passes and suitcases.
- Answer any questions the agent has about your trip.

E Family Trip

This family is going on a trip. These are pictures they take at the airport as they prepare to leave. On a separate piece of paper, write a paragraph about the family and the trip they're going on.

Include:
- Where they're going and when
- How they planned their trip
- How they booked it
- How they went through the airport

Unit 1
New People and Places

Lesson 1 Subject pronouns and *be*

We use pronouns to replace subjects in sentences and questions.

be questions	short answers	long answers and statements
Am I late?	Yes, I **am**. / No, I**'m not**.	Yes, I**'m** late. / No, I**'m not** late.
Is he / she / it from Europe?	Yes, he / she / it **is**. No, he / she / it **isn't**. No, he**'s** / she**'s** / it**'s not**.	Yes, he**'s** / she**'s** / it**'s** from Europe. No, he / she / it **isn't** from Europe. No, he**'s** / she**'s** / it**'s not** from Europe.
Are you / we / they riding a bike?	Yes, you / we / they **are**. No, you / we / they **aren't**.	Yes, you / we / they **are** riding a bike. No, you / we / they **aren't** riding a bike.

Lesson 2 *be* with *how* and adjectives; empty *it*

We use *how* and *be* to ask for information. We use adjectives to describe the subject.

How's your grandmother?   She's good!

be in *how* questions	
how + *be* + subject	How **are** you? How **is** your father? How **am** I doing?
How far / long / much / many + *be* + subject	How long **is** the train ride? How old **are** you?
adjectives after *be*	
subject + *be* + adjective	She**'s** sick. We**'re** tired. I**'m** great.
empty *it*	
Sentences about weather, times, days and dates, and distances often have an empty *it* subject. It's "empty" because it doesn't replace a noun.	
weather	A: How's the weather? B: It's a bad day. It's rainy.
time	A: What time is it? B: It's 4:00.
day/date	A: What day is it? / What's the date? B: It's Friday. / It's November 18.
distance	A: How far is it to the restaurant? B: It's five kilometers.

Lesson 3 *be* in wh- questions; demonstratives; possessive adjectives

Wh- words ask for specific information. Demonstratives and possessives say what person, place, or thing we are talking about. Demonstratives can be used either before a noun or alone.

be in *wh-* questions
Wh- word + *be* + S
Where am I right now? **What are** you eating? **Who is** that old man? **Why is** this movie bad?

possessive adjectives	
singular	**plural**
my sister **your** coffee **his/her** siblings **its** company	**our** computer **your** pencil **their** problems

demonstratives	
singular	**plural**
this pencil in my hand **that** computer on the desk	**these** pencils in my hand **those** computers on the desk

Lesson 4 *want (to)* and *would like (to)*

Want and *would like* say what we desire.

Use *want* and *would like* before a noun or *to* + verb. *Would like* is a little more formal than *want*.

want / *would like* + noun	*want to* / *would like to* + verb
Would like + noun is a more indirect and polite way of saying that you want something.	*Would like to* means *want to*. It is more indirect, so it is also used for wishes that cannot happen.
I **want** a job. / I **would like** a job. I **want** some food. / I **would like** some food.	I **want to** go to business school. I **would like** to go to business school. I **would like** to be a chef (but I can't cook).
To make short forms with *would like*, add -'*d* to the subject pronoun: I'*d*, you'*d*, he'*d*, she'*d*, it'*d*, we'*d*, they'*d*. I'**d like** to meet the professor. She'**d like** tea. We'**d like** to travel to Japan this year.	

Lesson 5 Questions with *be like*; adjectives

We use *be* + *like* and adjectives to ask and answer questions about people, places, and things.

In questions, use *What* + *be* + subject + *like?*
In sentences, the adjective comes after the subject + *be* and sometimes before a noun.

questions with *be like*	adjectives	
These questions ask you to describe a person or place.	You can describe things using adjectives. They can come after some verbs or before nouns.	
***What* + *be* verb + subject + *like* (+ extra information)?**	**S + V + adj.**	**(article +) adj. + N**
What**'s** your uncle **like**? What's the class **like**? What **are** your brothers **like** when they're together?	He's **nice** and **funny**. It's **interesting**. They're **loud** and **active**.	He's a **nice** man. It's an **interesting** class. They are **loud** guys.

Lesson 1 Simple present questions with *what* and *how*; intensifiers

We use *what* and *how* with present verbs to ask about people, places, and things. Intensifiers describe adjectives.

What/How + V + S (+ more information)?	
How are you?	I'm tired.
What's the apartment like?	It's large and clean.
What does Sara do?	She's a fashion designer.
What do you think of Texas?	I love it. / It's so hot. / It's good!
How does Alan like his job?	He says it's really interesting!

intensifiers: *so, quite, really, such*	
S + *be* + intensifier + adj.	**S + *be* verb + *such* (article) (adj.) + noun**
It's **really** fun.	It's **such** an old house.
She's **so** sick!	They're **such** bad players.
We're **quite** busy.	You're **such** a good father.

Lesson 2 Simple present yes/no questions; objects

We use *do* and *does* to ask and answer yes/no questions.

Put *do/does* before the subject + simple present verb (+ object) in a question.

yes/no questions	answers to yes/no questions
***Do(es)* + S + V (+ more information)?**	***Yes/No*, + S + *do(es)* (+ *not*) + V (+ more information).**
Do you like (pizza)? object	No, I **don't**. / No, I **don't** like pizza.
Do you have (a dog)? object	Yes, I **do**. / Yes, I **have** a dog.
Does it work?	No, it **doesn't**. / No, it **doesn't** work.
Does he have an apartment?	Yes, he **does**. / Yes, he **has** an apartment.
Do they have a sister?	No, they **don't**. / No, they **don't** have one.

Lesson 3 Questions with *any* and *how many*; object pronouns

We use *how many* and *any* to talk about the number of things or people. Object pronouns replace objects.

Object pronouns: *me, you, him, her, it, us, them*	Use an object pronoun only when the listener or reader knows what or who is being talked about.
You know **me**. Do you remember **me**?	The listener/reader knows *me*—*me* is the person talking.
He likes **that shirt**. Can he borrow **it**?	The listener knows *it* is *that shirt* —the speaker says *that shirt* in the previous sentence.
Is that **Mr. Smith**? Give **him** the gift.	The listener knows that *him* means *Mr. Smith*—the speaker mentions him in the previous sentence.

Do you have **any** pens?
   Yes, I do.
How many pens do you have?
   Only one.
	Sometimes *any* goes before a noun. It means more than zero. Answer *any questions* with yes/no. In questions, *how many* goes before a noun. Answer with a number.

Lesson 4 Questions with *why*; conjunction *because*; infinitives of purpose

We use *why* to ask for a reason. We use *because* and infinitives to explain a reason or purpose.

Use *why* at the start of a question. Use *because* + subject + verb. Put the infinitive of purpose after the main verb.

questions with *why*	*because*
Why asks for a reason.	You can use *because* + S + V to give a reason. Use it before or after another S + V. In speaking, it can be alone.
Why is she studying science? **Why** do you practice piano? **Why** does Jason work so much?	**Because** she wants to be a doctor. I practice **because** I want to play music well. **Because** he wants to save money, he always works so much.

infinitives	
infinitive = *to* + verb Sometimes *to* + verb gives a goal or a reason for doing something.	
She likes **to watch** movies. (object of the verb) He reads (in order) **to learn** a lot of information. (reason for reading) I eat well (in order) **to feel** healthy. (reason for eating well)	

Lesson 5 *should* and *have (got) to*

We use *should* to give advice. We use *have (got) to* when we talk about something that needs to happen.

Put *should* or *have (got) to* between the subject and base verb.

Peter shouldn't study engineering.
We've got to take a taxi.

should/shouldn't + base verb	
Should + verb is used to give advice or suggestions. It means something is a good idea. *should not* = *shouldn't*	You look tired. You **should** sleep. She **shouldn't** go to the game. She **should** study.

have to and *have got to*	
Have to + verb and *have got to* + verb mean *need to*. These expressions are stronger than *should*. They mean something is necessary. With *have got to*, the short form of *have/has* is often used.	I **have to** go to the doctor. I **have got to** go to the doctor. We**'ve got to** do our laundry. He**'s got to** take the train today. Rene**'s got to** get to math class.

Lesson 1 Simple present of *do* and *go*

We use *do* and *go* to talk about many activities.

Use *do* and *go* after *I, you, we*, and *they*. Use *does* and *goes* with the subjects *he, she* and *it*.

do	go
I / you / we / they **do**	I / you / we / they **go**
He / She / It does	He / She / It goes

useful expressions		
To talk about someone's occupation (reporter, student, secretary, etc.):	A: What **does** he **do**?	B: He **is** an engineer.
	A: What **do** you **do**?	B: I **work** for a school. I **am** a teacher.
To talk about which school someone attends and what someone studies:	A: Where **does** she **go**?	B: She **goes** to the University of Ottawa.
	A: What **do** you **study**?	B: I **study** accounting.

Lesson 2 Countable and uncountable nouns; *how many* and *how much*

A noun is either countable or uncountable. We use *how many/much* to talk about amounts of things. *Much* is usually used only in questions and negatives.

countable		uncountable	
determiners	example nouns	determiners	example nouns
a lot of many several few / a few	book**s** house**s** sister**s**	a lot of (not) much little / a little	homework music water

how many and how much	
Use *How many...?* when asking about something countable. Use *How much...?* when asking about something uncountable.	
How many...?	*How much...?*
How many cookies did you eat? **How many tickets** do you have?	**How much time** do you need? **How much coffee** did you drink?

Lesson 3 Articles

We use articles before specific and non-specific nouns.

Use *a* and *an* for non-specific nouns, *the* for specific nouns, and no article for general plural or uncountable nouns.

no article	a/an	the
Don't use an article before an uncountable or plural noun when talking generally.	Use *a* or *an* for *one* countable noun when you don't know *which* one.	Any noun can take *the* if there is enough information or context.
Elephants are big. (This is true for all elephants. *Elephants* is plural.)	*Please give me **an** umbrella.* (I want *any* umbrella.)	*Please give me **the** blue book*. (*Blue* tells you which one I want.)

places	
• Most proper nouns do not use an article, but some do—especially places that sound like plurals or unions (**the** *Philippines*, **the** *United States*), mountain ranges (**the** *Himalayas*), seas, and oceans (**the** *Pacific Ocean*). • Many places within a city or town take *the* (**the** *library*). We also use *the* with many natural areas (**the** *forest*). • Some places—*church, school, home* (and *hospital* in British English)—do not use an article when we are talking about the *function* of the place. (*He is in school* means he is studying.)	

Lesson 4 *there is* and *there are*; *some* and *any*

We use *there is/are* to talk about things that exist. Use *there is* + singular or uncountable nouns. Use *there are* + plural nouns.

there is	there are
Use *there is* for singular countable nouns and for uncountable nouns.	Use *there are* for plural countable nouns.
There is a car in front of the store. **Is there** a bus stop near here?	**Are there** any students here? **There are** many kinds of pasta.

some and any	
Some can be used with plural nouns or uncountable nouns, but *any* is usually used for negatives.	
There is **some** coffee in my office. There aren't **any** teachers in the library.	

Lesson 5 Proper nouns and capitalization

We use capital letters at the start of proper nouns.

Capitalize names of people, places, companies, streets, planets, days, months, books, movies, courses, etc.

DO capitalize:	examples
people's names	Bill Gates, Oprah Winfrey
companies' names	Microsoft, McDonald's
places	King Street, New York
days, months	Saturday, November
planets	Mars, Earth
specific courses	Introduction to Biology 101
books, movies, songs, articles	War and Peace, Pretty Woman

Titles of books, plays, songs, articles, works of art, etc., are proper nouns. They follow special capitalization rules:

• Always capitalize the first word in a title: *It's My Life*

• Capitalize all the other nouns, pronouns, verbs, adjectives, and adverbs: *Cool It; Fast Car*

• Do NOT capitalize articles (*a, an, the*), or common prepositions (*of, to, at*) except for the first word: *The Life of Pi; Of Mice and Men; She's the One*

Lesson 1 Prepositions of location

We use prepositions to describe where something is.
A preposition of location goes before a noun.

prepositions	examples
next to / beside near in front of behind between around inside outside on the right / left of across ___ from / opposite	The theater is **next to** the food court. There is a path **near** the courtyard. Let's meet **in front of** the dormitory. Do you know what's **behind** the garage? The office is **between** the entrance and the lab. There are a few shops **around** the campus. The bookstore is **inside** the arts building. A large fountain is **outside** my class. **On the left** of the student center, you can find the financial aid center. My classroom is **across** the hall **from** the housing office.

Lesson 2 Gerunds

We use verb + -ing as a noun. This is called a gerund.
Gerunds can be subjects or objects in a sentence.

Studying for chemistry is difficult.
I love playing baseball.

gerunds				
A gerund looks like a verb with an -ing ending, but it is used like a noun. It can be a subject, or it can be the object of verbs such as *like* or *avoid*.				
gerunds as subjects		**gerunds as objects**		
Cooking is fun. **Playing** cards bores me. **Smoking** scares me.		I enjoy **cooking**. I don't like **playing** cards. I quit **smoking**.		
some verbs with gerunds as objects				
like love hate	dislike enjoy prefer	avoid stop quit	consider start keep	continue practice imagine

Lesson 3 Present continuous and related time expressions

We use the present continuous to talk about actions happening right now or current and temporary actions.

Use subject + *be* + verb-*ing* to form the present continuous.

He's studying right now.
I'm living in Chicago this month.

statements: S + *be* + verb-*ing*...
They **are doing** research at the library right now. I'm not **enjoying** my part-time job this semester.
yes/no questions: *Be* + S + verb-*ing*...?
Are you **talking** to Brenda at the moment? **Is** she **taking** any art courses?
common time expressions
now, at the moment, right now, today, tonight, nowadays, this ___ (minute, morning, week, semester, year)

when and how to use present continuous
• To talk about what is happening right now. • To talk about something that is current and temporary. For example: *I'm learning to speak French—not at this moment, but these days. I'm living with a roommate this semester.* Both of these sentences bring attention to something current. • Present continuous sentences often use expressions about a current time.

Lesson 4 Present continuous in information questions

We use the present continuous with *Wh-* questions to get information about things.

Use *wh-* word + *be* + subject + verb-*ing* to form questions.

information questions: *Wh-* word + *be* + S + verb-*ing*...?		
questions	short answers	long answers
Where are we **going**?	To the cafeteria.	We're going **to the cafeteria**.
What books **is** she **reading**?	Romance and horror.	She's reading **romance and horror**.
How are you **feeling**?	Sick.	I'm feeling **sick**.
subject questions: *Who* + *be* + verb-*ing*...?		
Who's marking that exam?	Professor Williams (is).	**Professor Williams** is marking it.

Lesson 5 Simple present vs. present continuous

We use simple present to describe routines, general facts, or states. We use present continuous to describe actions happening now or current and temporary situations.

Use subject + verb or subject + *be* + verb-*ing*.

simple present	present continuous

Use for routines (the things people do every day or very often):
    I **wash** the dishes every day.
Use for facts that are generally true at all times:
    Doctors **help** patients.
	Use for something happening now:
	    Harry **is watching** his favorite TV show (right now).
	Use for something current and temporary:
	    I'm **taking** an exercise class this month.

stative verbs	
• Many verbs do not describe an action. Examples include *be* and *hate*. These verbs are called stative verbs. We usually use stative verbs in the simple present tense, NOT in the present continuous. • Stative verbs include most verbs that discuss what you know, think, or feel (*I love this cake.*), what you believe (*I don't believe her.*), what you see or hear (*I hear a noise!*), what you own (*I have a dog.*), or just ways of being. They don't discuss actions.	

Lesson 1 Comparison with adjectives

We use comparative adjectives to describe differences between people, places, and things.

Use adjectives with *more*, *-er*, and *less*, followed by *than*.

Do not use *than* with *not as … as.*

comparison to a higher degree			
one syllable adjective + -er	**adjectives ending in -y** *-y* to *-ier*	**two or more syllables** *more + adjective*	**irregular**
close – closer tall – taller fast – faster	rainy – rainier lovely – lovelier	**more** exciting **more** boring	good – **better** bad – **worse**
comparison to a lower degree			
option 1: *less + adjective*		option 2: *not as _____ as*	
less tiring less shy less happy less expensive		**not as** far as **not as** cheap as **not as** pretty as **not as** quiet as	

Lesson 2 Review of *-ing* forms and introduction to *-ing* adjectives

We use *-ing* forms as nouns, parts of verbs, and adjectives that describe a person, situation or thing that causes a feeling.

Put *-ing* after a verb. Use it before a noun or after a linking verb.

That movie was amazing!   *This is a boring lecture.*

The *-ing* form of a verb has three main uses:		
They can be used as **nouns**. For example: ***Running** is good for your health.* When an *-ing* form is used as a noun, it is called a **gerund**.	Present participles also help form **verbs**. For example: *I am **speaking** English.*	When present participles are used as **adjectives**, they describe a person, thing, or situation that causes a feeling. For example: *Sports are **exciting**.* Not all verbs can be used as *-ing* adjectives.
-ing adjectives		
-ing adjectives are also known as present participle adjectives. The present participle is formed by adding *-ing* to the root form of a verb: *see – seeing / talk – talking*		
Like most adjectives, *-ing* adjectives can be used before nouns or after linking verbs.		
Don't read that **boring** book. That new teacher seems **annoying**.		

Lesson 3 *How + adjective questions and answers*

We use *how* with adjectives for more information about a person, place, situation, or thing.

Begin a question with *How* + adjective. Answer directly, or with a comparative, superlative, or intensifier.

How large is the dorm room? It's very small.

How	adjective…?	Answer directly or with a comparative, a superlative, or an intensifier.
How	**cheap** is your rent?	It's only about $300 a month. (directly)
	good was the movie?	It was better than the one we saw last week. (comparative)
	big is their house?	It's the largest one in the neighborhood. (superlative)
	hard is the class?	It's quite difficult. (intensifier)

Lesson 4 Superlative adjectives

We use superlative adjectives to describe people, places, and things to the highest and lowest degree.

Use *-est*, *-iest*, *most*, and *least* with an adjective.

Susan lives in the closest apartment to the school.

superlatives for the highest degree			
one syllable adjective + -est	**adjectives ending in -y** *-y* to *-iest*	**two or more syllables** *most + adjective*	**irregular**
hard – hardest tall – tallest	healthy – healthiest silly – silliest	**most** difficult **most** exciting	good – **best** bad – **worst**
superlatives for the lowest degree			
least + adjective	**least** boring, **least** relaxing, **least** capable, **least** expensive		

Lesson 5 Linking verbs

These are non-action verbs that give information about a subject.

Linking verbs come before adjectives or nouns.

That music sounds terrible.   *Helen is a doctor.*

linking verbs
Linking verbs connect a subject with information about that subject. They are not action verbs. An adjective can follow a linking verb, and a noun can follow some linking verbs (*be, become, remain*). Some verbs are always linking verbs. Others can be both action verbs and linking verbs.
"true" linking verbs (verbs that only function as linking verbs)
be, become, seem: *He **is** happy.   She **seems** sad. We **are becoming** strong students.*
common verbs that can be action verbs or linking verbs
look, remain, smell, sound, taste, turn, stay, get, appear, feel, grow: *The students **look** excited.   This dinner **smells** wonderful. This window **feels** cold.*
action verbs vs. linking verbs
A linking verb can be followed directly by an adjective. • Action verb: *The cook **smells** the stew.* (The noun *stew* is the object of the verb *smells*.) • Linking verb: *The stew **smells** bad.* (*Bad* is an adjective.)

Lesson 1 Simple past of *be*

We use *be* in the past tense to ask and answer questions about a subject.

Use *was* with *I*, *he*, *she*, and *it*. Use *were* with *you*, *we*, and *they*.

Was it cheap? Yes, it was. / No, it wasn't.

simple present: *is/are*		simple past: *was/were*	
questions	answers	questions	answers
Is your new house small?	Yes, it **is**. No, it **isn't**.	**Was** your old house small?	Yes, it **was**. No, it **wasn't**.
Are your roommates fun?	Yes, they **are**. No, they **aren't**.	**Were** there lots of cafes near your old dormitory?	Yes, there **were**. No, there **weren't**.

Lesson 2 *there was/were*; conjunctions *or* and *but*

We use *there was/were* to describe what was in a certain place. We use *or* to list similar choices. We use *but* to compare opposite ideas.

Put a singular or uncountable noun after *there was*. Put a plural noun after *there were*. Put *or* between similar choices. Put *but* between opposite ideas.

Were there stores and restaurants nearby? No, there weren't any stores or restaurants, but there was a library.

there was / there were		
There was a bus stop next to my apartment.	**There wasn't** a lot of sunlight in the living room.	**Was there** a grocery store nearby?
There were many great shops there.	**There weren't** any museums nearby.	**Were there** restaurants in the area?
using *or*		using *but*
There wasn't a cinema **or** an art gallery in Paolo's neighborhood. There weren't any shops **or** cafés.		There was a library, **but** there wasn't a church. There weren't any subways, **but** there was a bus stop.

Lesson 3 Prepositions with time expressions (*in* / *on* / *at*)

Prepositions help describe when something happened, happens, or will happen.

Use *in*, *on*, or *at* in front of time words.

School ends in May.   The movie begins at 7:00 tonight.

in	*on*	*at*
the morning / the afternoon / the evening January, February, March, etc. spring, summer, fall, winter	the weekend Sunday, Monday, Tuesday, etc. a specific date (for example, May 4th, July 7th)	noon midnight night 6:00, 7:30, etc.
examples		
I drink tea **in** the morning. My sister is going to New York **on** the weekend. The basketball game starts **at** 6:30 p.m.		

Lesson 4 Simple past (regular verbs) and past time expressions

We use past verbs and time expressions to describe events that happened already.

Use verb + *-ed* for positives, *didn't* + base verb for negatives, and *did* + base verb for questions. Put past time expressions at the beginning or end of a sentence.

I visited Daniel two days ago.
Did Li cook dinner last night?

simple past (regular verbs): verb + *-ed*		
statements	negatives	yes/no questions
I He She It **called** Mary. We You They	I He She **did not** It **(didn't)** We **call** Mary. You / They	I he she **Did** it **call** Mary? we you they
past time expressions		
yesterday last week(end) / month / year last Friday two days / weeks / months / years ago		

Lesson 5 Simple past: irregular verbs

Some verbs have irregular forms when describing the past.

Use irregular past for positives, *didn't* + base verb for negatives, and *did* + base verb for questions.

Did you go to Tony's house? No, I didn't go. I went home.

simple past: irregular verbs			
wake – woke drink – drank get – got	take – took read – read make – made	leave – left have – had teach – taught	eat – ate go – went
statement		negative	
(subject)	**woke** up at 7:00.	(subject)	**did not (didn't) wake** up at 7:00.
question			
Did	(subject)	**wake** up at 7:00?	

Unit 7

Before the Trip

Lesson 1   Making suggestions

We make suggestions to share our ideas or advice.

To make a suggestion, you can use *let's* + verb + or *What about / How about* + verb + *-ing*?

Let's have pasta for dinner.

making suggestions using *let's*	making suggestions with *What about / How about* + verb + *-ing*
Use *let's* + the base form of the verb.	Use *what* or *how* + *about* + the *-ing* form of the verb.
Let's go home. **Let's check** the schedule.	**What about seeing** a movie tonight? **How about doing** a puzzle?

Note *Let's* is short for *Let us*, but don't say *Let us*. It's hardly ever used.

Lesson 2   Discussing the future; showing agreement

We use the present continuous to talk about a plan for the future.

To form the present continuous, use S + be + verb + *-ing*.

I am going to my mom's house for dinner.

present continuous with future meaning		
S + *be* + verb-*ing*		
I am going to college **in the fall.** **My girlfriend is visiting** me **next week.**		
subject pronoun	*be* verb	short form
I	am **verb** + *-ing*	I'm **verb** + *-ing*
you	are **verb** + *-ing*	you're **verb** + *-ing*
he / she / it	is **verb** + *-ing*	he's / she's / it's **verb** + *-ing*
we	are **verb** + *-ing*	we're **verb** + *-ing*
you (guys/all)	are **verb** + *-ing*	you're **verb** + *-ing*
they	are **verb** + *-ing*	they're **verb** + *-ing*

Note Some verbs do not use the continuous form.

Note We can agree with positive or negative statements.

To agree with a positive statement, say, "Me, too," or, "I do, too."

To agree with a negative statement, say, "Me neither," or "I don't either."

A: I love pizza.

B: I do, too.

agreement	
with positive statements	**with negative statements**
A: I love her dress. B: **Me too. / I do too!**	A: I don't like soda. B: **Me neither. / I don't either.**

Lesson 3   *can* for ability; *can* and *could* for possibility

We use *can* for ability or possibility. We use *could* for possibility.

Can and *could* go before bare infinitives or base verbs.

can for ability: *can* + verb	*can* and *could* for possibility: *can/could* + verb
Use *can* to talk about ability—things you're able to do.	Use *can* or *could* to talk about possibility in the present or the future. *Could* means the same as *can* in this context but is less direct.
I **can play tennis** well. He **can't cook** a good meal.	We **can/could go** out for pizza, or we **could/can order** in. We **could/can take** the train.

Lesson 4   *can* for offers and volunteering; *need to* for obligation

Can and *need to* can be used for offers, volunteering, or obligations.

Use S + *can* + verb or S + *need to* + verb.

I can help you study for your exam.

can for offers and volunteering S + *can* + verb	*need to* for obligation S + *need to* + verb
Use *can* to make offers or volunteer to do things.	Use *need to* like *have to* (See Unit 2 Lesson 5). Use it when you have an obligation (something you have to do).
I **can carry** your bags for you. I **can pay** for dinner tonight.	She **needs to study** for the quiz tomorrow. Do I **need to sign up** for the class?

Lesson 5   Imperatives

Use imperatives to give commands, make suggestions, give instructions, or encourage someone.

To form an imperative, use a base form verb or *do not / don't* + verb.

Don't touch that.

affirmative imperatives: verb (base form)	negative imperatives: *Do not / Don't* + verb
Take it easy. (suggestion/farewell) **Call** her back. (command/instruction) **Give** it to me. (command) **Turn** the page. (instruction)	**Don't press** the red button! (command) **Don't eat** the salad. (instruction) **Don't give** her your phone number.(command) **Don't worry** about it. (encouraging someone) **Don't drink** the water. (command)

Lesson 1 *Can* and *could* for offers and requests

We use *can* for offers and *can/could* for requests.

To form requests, permission, or offers, use:

Can I + verb…? / I can + verb or *Can/Could + S + verb*

Can I use your cell phone?

can for offers	can/could for requests
Can I + verb…? / I can + verb	**Can/Could + S + verb…?**
Can I bring you your wallet. **I can bring** you your wallet.	**Can/Could you tell** me where the bathroom is? A: **Can/Could I** use your flashlight, please? B: Sure.

Note *Could* is a little more polite than *can*.

Lesson 2 Questions with *Whose* and possessive pronouns

We use *whose* to ask who owns something. Possessive pronouns can answer those questions.

Whose + noun…?

Whose shoes are these? They're mine.

subject pronoun	possessive pronoun
I	mine
you	yours
he	his
she	hers
we	ours
they	theirs

questions with *whose*	possessive pronouns
Whose + noun…?	Possessive pronouns replace names or possessive adj. + noun. They describe ownership.
Whose hat is this? **Whose house** are we going to? **Whose backpacks** are these?	It's Sheila's. → It's **hers**. Let's go to your house. → Let's go to **yours**. They're my backpacks. → They're **mine**.

Lesson 3 Comparing with adverbs

Adverbs describe actions. We compare with adverbs to show differences in the way two things are done.

Adverbs often come after the verb in the sentence: *He walked **quickly** through the airport.*

Many adverbs are made by adding *-ly* to an adjective. To form the comparative of an *-ly* adverb, use *more +* adverb. But some words are the same in both adjective and adverb form *(early, fast)*. Their comparative adverb forms are the same as their comparative adjective forms (see Unit 5 Lesson 1). Other adverbs are irregular *(well, badly, far)*.

adverbs	comparative adverbs	examples
slowly	**more** slowly (than) / slow**er** (than)*	My English teacher speaks **more slowly than** my math teacher.
quickly	**more** quickly (than) / quick**er** (than)*	I can run **more quickly / quicker than** you!
early	earl**ier** (than)	Ben wakes up **earlier than** me.
fast	fast**er** (than)	Run **faster than** the dog!
well	**better** (than)	His health is **better than** before.
badly	**worse** (than)	A: I did **badly** on the exam. B: I did **worse than** you!
far	**farther** (than)	The school is **farther than** the supermarket.

Note *Quick* and *slow* are sometimes used as adverbs.

Lesson 4 Superlative adverbs; *how* + adverb

Superlative adverbs compare adverbs to the highest degree.

To form the superlative of an *-ly* adverb, use *the most +* adverb. Adverbs with irregular comparative forms also have irregular superlative forms. (See Lesson 3 of this unit.)

adverbs	superlative adverbs	examples
slowly	the **most** slowly / the slow**est**	My English teacher speaks **the most slowly** out of all my teachers.
quickly	the **most** quickly / the quick**est**	I can run **the most quickly / the quickest**!
early	the earl**iest**	Daniel wakes up **the earliest**.
fast	the fast**est**	The lion runs **the fastest**.
well	the **best**	His health is **the best** it's ever been.
badly	the **worst**	I failed the exam. I did **the worst**.
far	the **farthest**	The gym is **the farthest** from school.

Lesson 5 *have + O + to* verb; time expressions

Use *have + O* to talk about an object that you possess.

Use *have to +* verb to talk about something that is important to do.

Use *have + O + to* verb to talk about things that you have and that you can do or use.

have + O	have to + verb	have + O + to verb
I **have a dog.** She **has a pencil.**	I **have to do** my job. He **has to go** to his mom's house.	I **have work to finish.** She **has food to eat.**

You use time expressions to talk about when something happens (or happened) in the past, present, or future.

time expressions about the past	time expressions about the present	time expressions about the future
yesterday last night	on Tuesdays between 8 and 9 p.m.	tomorrow in two hours
We had dinner **last night.**	She studies **on Tuesdays.**	Our flight leaves **in two hours.**

Unit 1
New People and Places

Lesson 1
train station
head
get married
get together
Good seeing you.
Good to see you.
Nice meeting you.
Nice to meet you.
Thanks for the ride.
This is…

Lesson 2
contest
newspaper
professional
reporter
cook
own
win
future
by the way
Congratulations.
I'm awesome.
I'm fine / all right.
I'm good / great.
I'm great.
I'm not bad.
I'm okay.
I'm sick.
I'm tired.
If you don't mind my
    asking…

Lesson 3
boss
business
CEO
company
coworker
employee
intern
meeting
secretary
supervisor
Have a seat.

Lesson 4
advice
career
clothes
counselor
fashion designer
pop star

semester
draw
graduate
creative
pop (or popular)

Lesson 5
area
bay
bridge
country
country music
hometown
mountain
state
beautiful
famous
rural
urban

Unit 2
Small Talk

Lesson 1
degree(s)
Celsius
Fahrenheit
forecast
season
temperature
weather
clear
cloudy
dry
high
humid
low
so
huh

Lesson 2
architect
engineering
major
mechanic
minor
software
tuition
choose
full-time
part-time

Lesson 3
only child
sibling
laugh
smile

fat
friendly
intelligent
opposite
serious
shy
thin

Lesson 4
foreigner
goal
pilot
attend
move
reach
curious
difficult
international
reach a goal
set a goal
talk with

Lesson 5
algebra
champion
grade
half
league
winner
cheer
miss
pitch
big

Unit 3
Your University

Lesson 1
primary school
elementary school
secondary school
middle school
high school
graduate/grad
freshman
sophomore
junior
senior
degree
engineer
occupation
go to
class of
What do you do?

Lesson 2
business administration

cosmetology
department
elementary education
fine arts
mathematics
nursing
physical education
software engineering

Lesson 3
director
film school
graduate school
junior college
law school
medical school
trade school
vocational school
which

Lesson 4
admissions building
dormitory (dorm)
fountain
garden
quad
stadium
swimming pool
theater
huge

Lesson 5
expenses
fee(s)
housing
loan
meal plan
scholarship
afford
cheap
expensive
not bad
reasonable
It costs too much.
It doesn't cost much.

Unit 4
College Life

Lesson 1
academic center
administration building
athletic center
auditorium
concert hall
courtyard
financial aid center

food court
garage
housing office
laboratory (lab)
student center
academic
next to / beside
near
in front of
behind
between
around
inside
outside
on the right / left of
across from / opposite

Lesson 2

lecture
avoid
consider
continue
dislike
enjoy
hate
imagine
keep
like
love
practice
prefer
quit
start
stop
doing experiments
doing research
solving problems
taking notes

Lesson 3

club
current event
extracurricular activity
roommate
skill
chat
improve
join
currently
at the moment
get along
these days

Lesson 4

agriculture
assignment
elective
industry

presentation
topic
historical
keep up

Lesson 5

event
routine
involving
special
always
usually
sometimes
occasionally
often
hardly ever
never
per
participate (in)
take part (in)

Unit 5

A New Place

Lesson 1

landlord
(by) bicycle
(by) bike
(by) boat
(by) car
(by) plane
(by) subway
(by) taxi
(by) train
on foot (walk)

Lesson 2

amazing
annoying
boring
confusing
exciting
interesting
relaxing
tiring
on time

Lesson 3

one block
go straight
turn left
turn right
across the street from
on the corner
or so

Lesson 4

heat
lights
furnished
unfurnished
apartment (apt)
available (avail)
bedroom (bdrm)
immediately (immed)
included (incl)
month (mth)
utilities (util)

Lesson 5

afraid
angry
happy
nervous
sad
surprised
tired
upset
lots of

Unit 6

At Home

Lesson 1

balcony
bathtub
burner
ceiling fan
closet
home office
rug
sink
stove
view

Lesson 2

bakery
bank
clothing store
gallery
gym
market
museum
park
pharmacy
supermarket
next door

Lesson 3

evening
at 10:35
at 2 o'clock
at night
on Monday, Tuesday, etc.

on the weekend
in January, February, etc.
in the afternoon
in the evening
in the morning
years old

Lesson 4

act up
drop (someone) off
kick (someone) out
look after
look in on
look up

Lesson 5

ran
ate breakfast
drank coffee
got home
had lunch
left for school
made dinner
read news
took the subway
went to the gym
woke up
typical

Unit 7

Before the Trip

Lesson 1

camel
desert
jungle
option
thrill-seeker
tour
Africa
Costa Rica
Mexico
Morocco
explore
check online
off the beaten path
I do too.
Me too.

Lesson 2

China
India
hate
spicy
yum
extreme heat
good point

Lesson 3
ad
adventure
fan
hike
river
riverboat
trail
fantastic
incredible

Lesson 4
date
deal
ticket
travel agency
book
compare
specific
quick
ASAP
in person

Lesson 5
airport
aisle
aisle seat
middle seat
overhead compartment
passport
window seat
click
print
afraid of heights

Unit 8
At the Airport

Lesson 1
baggage cart
check-in counter
escalator
gate
terminal
late
lost
check in

Lesson 2
boarding pass
carry-on
flight
scale
suitcase
check
pass

heavy
Do you mind -ing?
Here you go.

Lesson 3
bin
conveyor belt
duty-free shop
metal detector
anxious
excited
stressed
terrified

Lesson 4
line
liquid
passenger
millimeter (ml)
liter (l)
centimeter (cm)
meter (m)
kilometer (km)
FAQ (Frequently Asked
  Questions)
follow
measure
process

Lesson 5
celebrity
departure board
gossip
magazine
delayed
flip through